EVOLVE

STUDENT'S BOOK

Ben Goldstein and Ceri Jones

4A

CAMBRIDGE
UNIVERSITY PRESS

CAMBRIDGE
UNIVERSITY PRESS

University Printing House, Cambridge CB2 8BS, United Kingdom

One Liberty Plaza, 20th Floor, New York, NY 10006, USA

477 Williamstown Road, Port Melbourne, VIC 3207, Australia

314–321, 3rd Floor, Plot 3, Splendor Forum, Jasola District Centre, New Delhi – 110025, India

79 Anson Road, #06–04/06, Singapore 079906

Cambridge University Press is part of the University of Cambridge.

It furthers the University's mission by disseminating knowledge in the pursuit of education, learning, and research at the highest international levels of excellence.

www.cambridge.org
Information on this title: www.cambridge.org/9781108405096

First published 2019

20 19 18 17 16 15 14 13 12 11 10 9 8 7 6 5 4 3 2

Printed in Great Britain by CPI Group (UK) Ltd, Croydon CR0 4YY

A catalogue record for this publication is available from the British Library

ISBN 978-1-108-40531-7 Student's Book
ISBN 978-1-108-40509-6 Student's Book A
ISBN 978-1-108-40923-0 Student's Book B
ISBN 978-1-108-40532-4 Student's Book with Practice Extra
ISBN 978-1-108-40510-2 Student's Book with Practice Extra A
ISBN 978-1-108-40925-4 Student's Book with Practice Extra B
ISBN 978-1-108-40901-8 Workbook with Audio
ISBN 978-1-108-40874-5 Workbook with Audio A
ISBN 978-1-108-41194-3 Workbook with Audio B
ISBN 978-1-108-40518-8 Teacher's Edition with Test Generator
ISBN 978-1-108-41071-7 Presentation Plus
ISBN 978-1-108-41204-9 Class Audio CDs
ISBN 978-1-108-40795-3 Video Resource Book with DVD
ISBN 978-1-108-41449-4 Full Contact with DVD
ISBN 978-1-108-41155-4 Full Contact A with DVD
ISBN 978-1-108-41417-3 Full Contact B with DVD

Additional resources for this publication at www.cambridge.org/evolve

ACKNOWLEDGMENTS

The *Evolve* publishers would like to thank the following individuals and institutions who have contributed their time and insights into the development of the course:

Maria Araceli Hernández Tovar, Instituto Tecnológico Superior de San Luis Potosí, Capital, Mexico; Kayla M. Briggs, Hoseo University, South Korea; Lenise Butler, Laureate, Mexico; Aslı Derin Anaç, İstanbul Bilgi University, Turkey; Roberta Freitas, IBEU, Rio de Janeiro, Brazil; José Manuel Cuin Jacuinde, Coordinación de Lenguas Extranjeras del Instituto Tecnológico de Morelia, Mexico; Thomas Christian Keller, Universidad de las Américas, Chile; Daniel Lowe, Lowe English Services, Panama; Ivanova Monteros, Universidad Tecnológica Equinoccial, Ecuador; Daniel Nowatnick, USA; Diego Ribeiro Santos, Universidade Anhembri Morumbi, São Paulo, Brazil; Jason Williams, Notre Dame Seishin University, Japan; Matthew Wilson, Miyagi University, Japan; Yudy Rios, Universidad Pedagógica Nacional, Colombia

To our student contributors, who have given us their ideas and their time, and who appear throughout this book:

Andres Ramírez, Mexico; Alessandra Avelar, Brazil; Nicolle Juliana Torres Sierra, Colombia; Ouattara Maryne Soukeina, USA; Seung Geyong Yang, South Korea; Tayra Laritza Lacayo Sanchez, Honduras.

And special thanks to Katy Simpson, teacher and writer at *myenglishvoice.com*

Authors' Acknowledgments:

A special thanks to all the editorial team, particularly Dena Daniel, whose patience and professionalism helped make this project a pleasure to work on.

The authors and publishers acknowledge the following sources of copyright material and are grateful for the permissions granted. While every effort has been made, it has not always been possible to identify the sources of all the material used, or to trace all copyright holders. If any omissions are brought to our notice, we will be happy to include the appropriate acknowledgements on reprinting and in the next update to the digital edition, as applicable.

Text

p. 54: Logo of Social Bite. Copyright © Social Bite Fund. Reproduced with kind permission; p. 55: Logo of World Wildlife Fund. Copyright © 1986 Panda symbol WWF – World Wide Fund for Nature. Reproduced with kind permission; p. 55: Logo of Doctors Without Borders. Copyright © Doctors Without Borders/Médecins Sans Frontières (MSF). Reproduced with kind permission; p. 60: Text about The City Repair Project. Reproduced with kind permission of The City Repair.

Photographs

B = Below, BC = Below Centre, BG = Background, BL = Below Left, BR = Below Right, CL = Centre Left, CR = Centre Right, TC = Top Centre, TL = Top Left, TR = Top Right.

The following photographs are sourced from Getty Images.

p. xvi (TR): asiseeit/E+; p. xvi (BL): vlada_maestro/iStock/Getty Images Plus; p. 1, p. 36 (BR): Chris Ryan/Caiaimage; p. 2 (photo a): Nicola Tree/The Image Bank; p. 2 (photo b): PeopleImages/iStock/Getty Images Plus; p. 3 (photo c): Sigrid Gombert/Cultura; p. 3: artpartner-images/Photographer's Choice; p. 4: Klaus Vedfelt/Taxi; p. 5: DivVector/DigitalVision Vectors; p. 6, p. 21 (CR), p. 53: Hero Images; p. 7: Paul Archuleta/FilmMagic; p. 8: sturti/E+; p. 9: Joe Raedle/Getty Images News; pp. 10, 20, 30, 42, 52, 62: Tom Merton/Caiaimage; p. 10 (tourist): Andrew Peacock/Lonely Planet Images; p. 11: nedomacki/iStock/Getty Images Plus; p. 12: Neilson Barnard/Getty Images Entertainment; p. 13: Mint Images RF; p. 14 (barbeque): Teresa Miller/EyeEm; p. 14 (boil): UllrichG/iStock/Getty Images Plus; p. 14 (chop): Chris Cole/DigitalVision; p. 14 (stir): tzahiV/iStock/Getty Images Plus; p. 14 (fry): Dorling Kindersley; p. 14 (rinse): Sidekick/iStock/Getty Images Plus; p. 15: ma-k/E+; p. 16: Maskot; p. 17: EddieHernandezPhotography/iStock/Getty Images Plus; p. 18 (photo 1): Foodcollection RF; p. 18 (photo 2): KyleNelson/E+; p. 20, p. 30 (couple): Westend61; p. 21: Anouk de Maar/Cultura; p. 22 (TR): vgajic/E+; p. 23: Nomad/E+; p. 24: Ezra Bailey/Taxi; p. 25: Jan Sandvik/EyeEm; p. 26: Rudolf Vlcek/Moment Open; p. 27: NoDerog/iStock/Getty Images Plus; p. 28 (TL): Víctor Del Pino/EyeEm; p. 28 (TC): Maximilian Stock Ltd./Photolibrary; p. 28 (TR): inhauscreative/E+; p. 29: Logorilla/DigitalVision Vectors; p. 30 (CL): Hussein Fardin Fard/EyeEm; p. 30 (CR): Chalabala/iStock/Getty Images Plus; p. 32: Zigy Kaluzny-Charles Thatcher/The Image Bank; p. 33: Maremagnum/Photolibrary; p. 35: SERGEI SUPINSKY/AFP; p. 36 (BL): Fotos International/Archive Photos; p. 36 (BC): Ethan Miller/Getty Images Entertainment; p. 36 (TR): BANARAS KHAN/AFP; p. 38: djedzura/iStock/Getty Images Plus; p. 40 (cowboy): Vicki Jauron, Babylon and Beyond Photography/Moment; p. 40 (photo a): Creative Crop/Photodisc; p. 40 (photo b): Miguel Schincariol/AFP; p. 42 LauriPatterson p. 43: LuminaStock/iStock/Getty Images Plus; p. 47: Jo-Ann Richards/First Light; p. 48: Henn Photography/Cultura; p. 50: fotofrog/iStock/Getty Images Plus; p. 51: Jordan Siemens/Taxi; p. 52 (man): GeorgeRudy/iStock/Getty Images Plus; p. 52 (woman): pablocalvog/iStock/Getty Images Plus; p. 56: AndreyPopov/iStock/Getty Images Plus; p. 58: skynesher/iStock/Getty Images Plus; p. 59: Johner Images; p.62 (CL): Phil Clarke Hill/In Pictures; p. 62 (TL): Mario Tama/Getty Images News; p. 64: UpperCut Images;

Below photographs are sourced from other libraries:

p. 45 (Manuela Saenz): Colport/Alamy Stock Photo; p. 60: © Anton Legoo, Portland Street Art Alliance; p.61: ©VERDEVERTICAL. Reproduced with kind permission.

Front cover photography by Alija/E+/Getty Images.

Illustrations by Ana Djordjevic (Astound US) pp. 157, 159; Lyn Dylan (Sylvie Poggio) pp. 157, 159; David Eaton (ODI) pp. 14–15.

Audio production by CityVox, New York.

EVOLVE

SPEAKING MATTERS

EVOLVE is a six-level American English course for adults and young adults, taking students from beginner to advanced levels (CEFR A1 to C1).

Drawing on insights from language teaching experts and real students, EVOLVE is a general English course that gets students speaking with confidence.

This student-centered course covers all skills and focuses on the most effective and efficient ways to make progress in English.

Confidence in teaching.

Joy in learning.

Better Learning WITH EVOLVE

Better Learning is our simple approach where insights we've gained from research have helped shape content that drives results. Language evolves, and so does the way we learn. This course takes a flexible, student-centered approach to English language teaching.

Meet our student contributors

Videos and ideas from real students feature throughout the Student's Book.

Our student contributors describe themselves in three words.

SEUNG GEYOUNG YANG

Happy, creative
Myongji University, South Korea

ANDRES RAMÍREZ FABIAN

Friendly, happy, funny
Instituto Tecnológico de Morelia, México

OUATTARA MARYNE SOUKEINA

Friendly, perfectionist, creative
Educational Language Services, USA

ALESSANDRA AVELAR

Creative, positive, funny
Faculdade ICESP, Águas Claras, Brazil

TAYRA LARITZA LACAYO SANCHEZ

Tenacious, oustanding, curious
La universidad global de Honduras

NICOLLE JULIANA TORRES SIERRA

Passionate, Friendly, committed
Centro Colombo Americano, Colombia

Student-generated content

EVOLVE is the first course of its kind to feature real student-generated content. We spoke to over 2,000 students from all over the world about the topics they would like to discuss in English and in what situations they would like to be able to speak more confidently.

The ideas are included throughout the Student's Book and the students appear in short videos responding to discussion questions.

INSIGHT

Research shows that achievable speaking role models can be a powerful motivator.

CONTENT

Bite-sized videos feature students talking about topics in the Student's Book.

RESULT

Students are motivated to speak and share their ideas.

"It's important to provide learners with interesting or stimulating topics."

Teacher, Mexico (Global Teacher Survey, 2017)

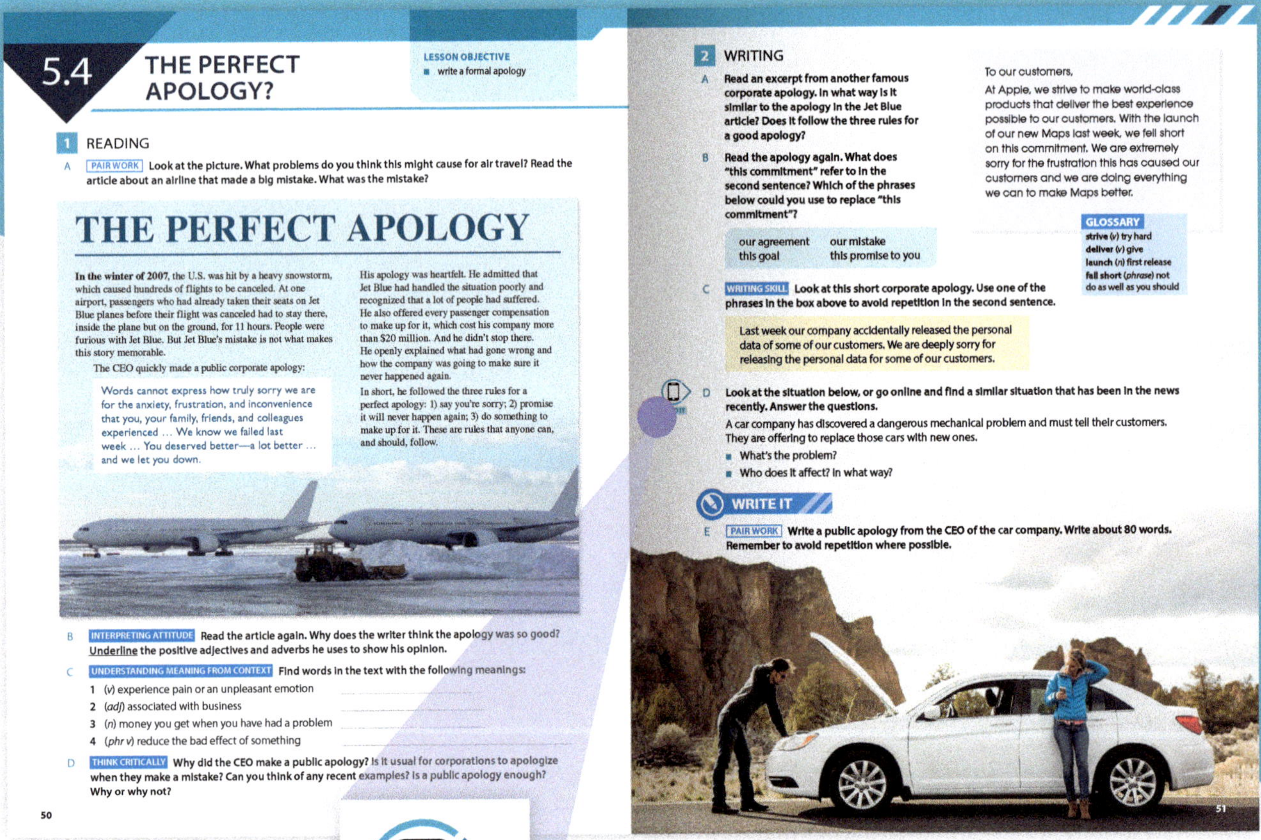

5.4 THE PERFECT APOLOGY?

LESSON OBJECTIVE
- write a formal apology

1 READING

A PAIR WORK Look at the picture. What problems do you think this might cause for air travel? Read the article about an airline that made a big mistake. What was the mistake?

THE PERFECT APOLOGY

In the winter of 2007, the U.S. was hit by a heavy snowstorm, which caused hundreds of flights to be canceled. At one airport, passengers who had already taken their seats on Jet Blue planes before their flight was canceled had to stay there, inside the plane but on the ground, for 11 hours. People were furious with Jet Blue. But Jet Blue's mistake is not what makes this story memorable.

The CEO quickly made a public corporate apology:

Words cannot express how truly sorry we are for the anxiety, frustration, and inconvenience that you, your family, friends, and colleagues experienced … We know we failed last week … You deserved better—a lot better … and we let you down.

His apology was heartfelt. He admitted that Jet Blue had handled the situation poorly and recognized that a lot of people had suffered. He also offered every passenger compensation to make up for it, which cost his company more than $20 million. And he didn't stop there. He openly explained what had gone wrong and how the company was going to make sure it never happened again.

In short, he followed the three rules for a perfect apology: 1) say you're sorry; 2) promise it will never happen again; 3) do something to make up for it. These are rules that anyone can, and should, follow.

B INTERPRETING ATTITUDE Read the article again. Why does the writer think the apology was so good? Underline the positive adjectives and adverbs he uses to show his opinion.

C UNDERSTANDING MEANING FROM CONTEXT Find words in the text with the following meanings:

1 (*v*) experience pain or an unpleasant emotion ______
2 (*adj*) associated with business ______
3 (*n*) money you get when you have had a problem ______
4 (*phr v*) reduce the bad effect of something ______

D THINK CRITICALLY Why did the CEO make a public apology? Is it usual for corporations to apologize when they make a mistake? Can you think of any recent examples? Is a public apology enough? Why or why not?

50

2 WRITING

A Read an excerpt from another famous corporate apology. In what way is it similar to the apology in the Jet Blue article? Does it follow the three rules for a good apology?

B Read the apology again. What does "this commitment" refer to in the second sentence? Which of the phrases below could you use to replace "this commitment"?

our agreement	our mistake
this goal	this promise to you

To our customers,

At Apple, we strive to make world-class products that deliver the best experience possible to our customers. With the launch of our new Maps last week, we fell short on this commitment. We are extremely sorry for the frustration this has caused our customers and we are doing everything we can to make Maps better.

GLOSSARY
strive (*v*) try hard
deliver (*v*) give
launch (*n*) first release
fall short (*phrase*) not do as well as you should

C WRITING SKILL Look at this short corporate apology. Use one of the phrases in the box above to avoid repetition in the second sentence.

Last week our company accidentally released the personal data of some of our customers. We are deeply sorry for releasing the personal data for some of our customers.

D Look at the situation below, or go online and find a similar situation that has been in the news recently. Answer the questions.

A car company has discovered a dangerous mechanical problem and must tell their customers. They are offering to replace those cars with new ones.

- What's the problem?
- Who does it affect? In what way?

WRITE IT

E PAIR WORK Write a public apology from the CEO of the car company. Write about 80 words. Remember to avoid repetition where possible.

51

Find it

INSIGHT

Research with hundreds of teachers and students across the globe revealed a desire to expand the classroom and bring the real world in.

CONTENT

Find it are smartphone activities that allow students to bring live content into the class and personalize the learning experience with research and group activities.

RESULT

Students engage in the lesson because it is meaningful to them.

Designed for success

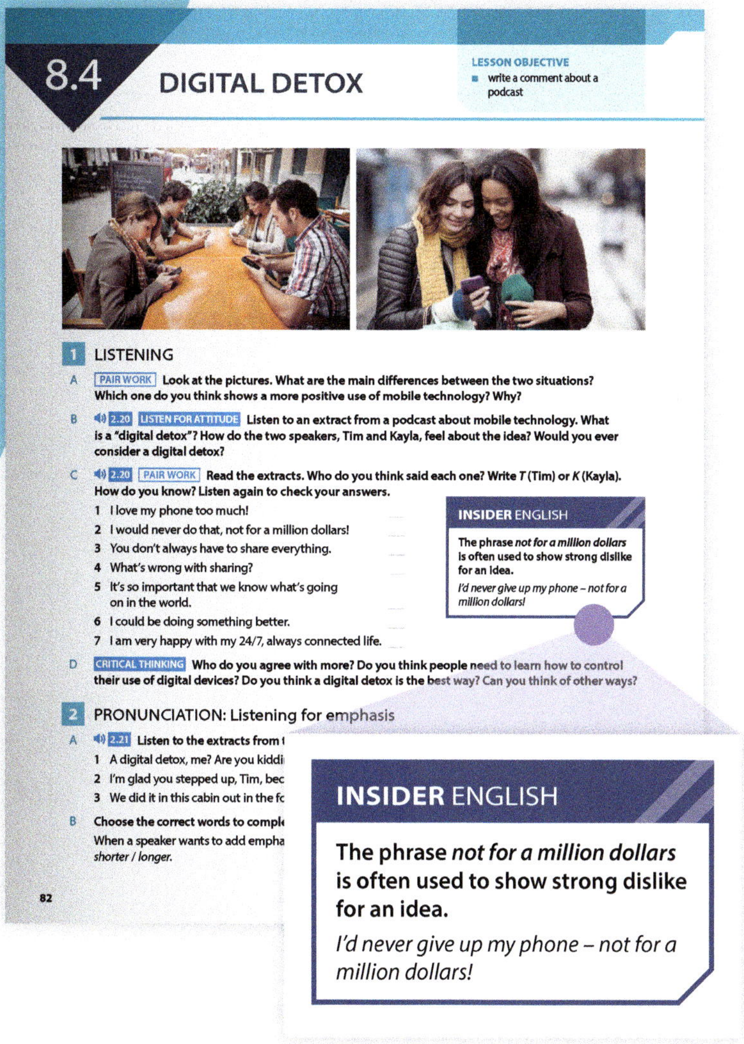

8.4 DIGITAL DETOX

LESSON OBJECTIVE
- write a comment about a podcast

1 LISTENING

A PAIR WORK Look at the pictures. What are the main differences between the two situations? Which one do you think shows a more positive use of mobile technology? Why?

B 2.20 LISTEN FOR ATTITUDE Listen to an extract from a podcast about mobile technology. What is a "digital detox"? How do the two speakers, Tim and Kayla, feel about the idea? Would you ever consider a digital detox?

C 2.20 PAIR WORK Read the extracts. Who do you think said each one? Write *T* (Tim) or *K* (Kayla). How do you know? Listen again to check your answers.

1 I love my phone too much! ___
2 I would never do that, not for a million dollars! ___
3 You don't always have to share everything. ___
4 What's wrong with sharing? ___
5 It's so important that we know what's going on in the world. ___
6 I could be doing something better. ___
7 I am very happy with my 24/7, always connected life. ___

INSIDER ENGLISH

The phrase *not for a million dollars* is often used to show strong dislike for an idea.

I'd never give up my phone – not for a million dollars!

D CRITICAL THINKING Who do you agree with more? Do you think people need to learn how to control their use of digital devices? Do you think a digital detox is the best way? Can you think of other ways?

2 PRONUNCIATION: Listening for emphasis

A 2.21 Listen to the extracts from t

1 A digital detox, me? Are you kiddi

2 I'm glad you stepped up, Tim, bec

3 We did it in this cabin out in the fc

B Choose the correct words to compl

When a speaker wants to add empha

shorter / longer.

82

INSIDER ENGLISH

The phrase *not for a million dollars* is often used to show strong dislike for an idea.

I'd never give up my phone – not for a million dollars!

Pronunciation

INSIGHT

Research shows that only certain aspects of pronunciation actually affect comprehensibility and inhibit communication.

CONTENT

EVOLVE focuses on the aspects of pronunciation that most affect communication.

RESULT

Students understand more when listening and can be clearly understood when they speak.

Insider English

INSIGHT

Even in a short exchange, idiomatic language can inhibit understanding.

CONTENT

Insider English focuses on the informal language and colloquial expressions frequently found in everyday situations.

RESULT

Students are confident in the real world.

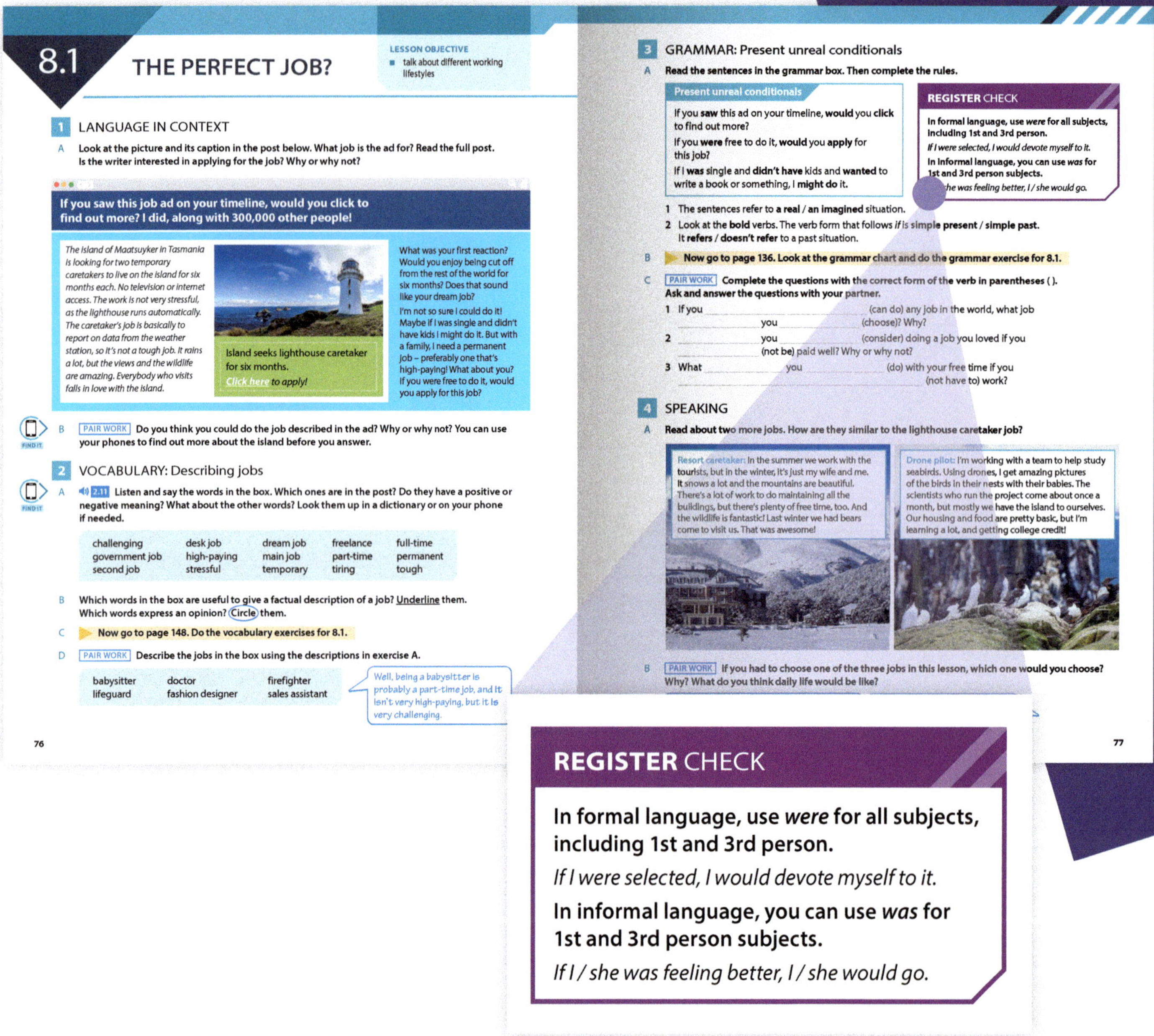

8.1 THE PERFECT JOB?

LESSON OBJECTIVE
- talk about different working lifestyles

1 LANGUAGE IN CONTEXT

A Look at the picture and its caption in the post below. What job is the ad for? Read the full post. Is the writer interested in applying for the job? Why or why not?

If you saw this job ad on your timeline, would you click to find out more? I did, along with 300,000 other people!

The island of Maatsuyker in Tasmania is looking for two temporary caretakers to live on the island for six months each. No television or internet access. The work is not very stressful, as the lighthouse runs automatically. The caretaker's job is basically to report on data from the weather station, so it's not a tough job. It rains a lot, but the views and the wildlife are amazing. Everybody who visits falls in love with the island.

Island seeks lighthouse caretaker for six months.
Click here to apply!

What was your first reaction? Would you enjoy being cut off from the rest of the world for six months? Does that sound like your dream job?
I'm not so sure I could do it! Maybe if I was single and didn't have kids I might do it. But with a family, I need a permanent job – preferably one that's high-paying! What about you? If you were free to do it, would you apply for this job?

B PAIR WORK Do you think you could do the job described in the ad? Why or why not? You can use your phones to find out more about the island before you answer.

2 VOCABULARY: Describing jobs

A 2.11 Listen and say the words in the box. Which ones are in the post? Do they have a positive or negative meaning? What about the other words? Look them up in a dictionary or on your phone if needed.

challenging	desk job	dream job	freelance	full-time
government job	high-paying	main job	part-time	permanent
second job	stressful	temporary	tiring	tough

B Which words in the box are useful to give a factual description of a job? Underline them. Which words express an opinion? Circle them.

C Now go to page 148. Do the vocabulary exercises for 8.1.

D PAIR WORK Describe the jobs in the box using the descriptions in exercise A.

babysitter	doctor	firefighter
lifeguard	fashion designer	sales assistant

Well, being a babysitter is probably a part-time job, and it isn't very high-paying, but it is very challenging.

76

3 GRAMMAR: Present unreal conditionals

A Read the sentences in the grammar box. Then complete the rules.

Present unreal conditionals

If you **saw** this ad on your timeline, **would** you **click** to find out more?
If you **were** free to do it, **would** you **apply** for this job?
If I **was** single and **didn't have** kids and **wanted** to write a book or something, I **might do** it.

1 The sentences refer to **a real / an imagined** situation.
2 Look at the **bold** verbs. The verb form that follows *if* is **simple present / simple past**. It **refers / doesn't refer** to a past situation.

B Now go to page 136. Look at the grammar chart and do the grammar exercise for 8.1.

C PAIR WORK Complete the questions with the correct form of the verb in parentheses ( ). Ask and answer the questions with your partner.

1 If you ________ (can do) any job in the world, what job ________ you ________ (choose)? Why?
2 ________ you ________ (consider) doing a job you loved if you ________ (not be) paid well? Why or why not?
3 What ________ you ________ (do) with your free time if you ________ (not have to) work?

4 SPEAKING

A Read about two more jobs. How are they similar to the lighthouse caretaker job?

Resort caretaker: In the summer we work with the tourists, but in the winter, it's just my wife and me. It snows a lot and the mountains are beautiful. There's a lot of work to do maintaining all the buildings, but there's plenty of free time, too. And the wildlife is fantastic! Last winter we had bears come to visit us. That was awesome!

Drone pilot: I'm working with a team to help study seabirds. Using drones, I get amazing pictures of the birds in their nests with their babies. The scientists who run the project come about once a month, but mostly we have the island to ourselves. Our housing and food are pretty basic, but I'm learning a lot, and getting college credit!

B PAIR WORK If you had to choose one of the three jobs in this lesson, which one would you choose? Why? What do you think daily life would be like?

77

REGISTER CHECK

In formal language, use *were* for all subjects, including 1st and 3rd person.

If I were selected, I would devote myself to it.

In informal language, you can use *was* for 1st and 3rd person subjects.

If I / she was feeling better, I / she would go.

Register check

INSIGHT

Teachers report that their students often struggle to master the differences between written and spoken English.

CONTENT

Register check draws on research into the Cambridge English Corpus and highlights potential problem areas for learners.

RESULT

Students transition confidently between written and spoken English and recognize different levels of formality as well as when to use them appropriately.

"The presentation is very clear and there are plenty of opportunities for student practice and production."

Jason Williams, Teacher, Notre Dame Seishin University, Japan

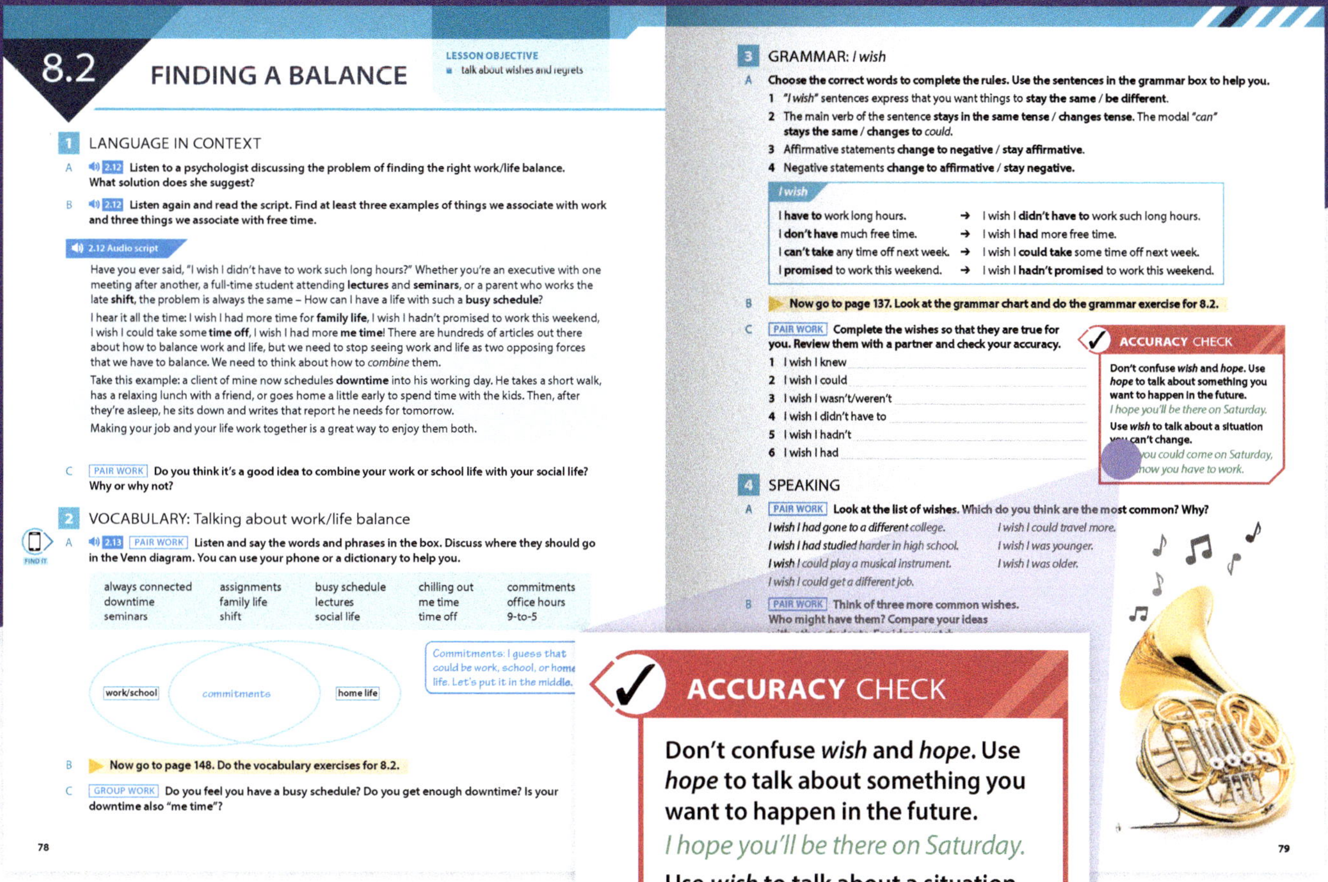

8.2 FINDING A BALANCE

LESSON OBJECTIVE
- talk about wishes and regrets

1 LANGUAGE IN CONTEXT

A 2.12 Listen to a psychologist discussing the problem of finding the right work/life balance. What solution does she suggest?

B 2.12 Listen again and read the script. Find at least three examples of things we associate with work and three things we associate with free time.

2.12 Audio script

Have you ever said, "I wish I didn't have to work such long hours?" Whether you're an executive with one meeting after another, a full-time student attending **lectures** and **seminars**, or a parent who works the late **shift**, the problem is always the same – How can I have a life with such a **busy schedule**?

I hear it all the time: I wish I had more time for **family life**, I wish I hadn't promised to work this weekend, I wish I could take some **time off**, I wish I had more **me time**! There are hundreds of articles out there about how to balance work and life, but we need to stop seeing work and life as two opposing forces that we have to balance. We need to think about how to *combine* them.

Take this example: a client of mine now schedules **downtime** into his working day. He takes a short walk, has a relaxing lunch with a friend, or goes home a little early to spend time with the kids. Then, after they're asleep, he sits down and writes that report he needs for tomorrow.

Making your job and your life work together is a great way to enjoy them both.

C PAIR WORK Do you think it's a good idea to combine your work or school life with your social life? Why or why not?

2 VOCABULARY: Talking about work/life balance

A 2.13 PAIR WORK Listen and say the words and phrases in the box. Discuss where they should go in the Venn diagram. You can use your phone or a dictionary to help you.

always connected, downtime, seminars, assignments, family life, shift, busy schedule, lectures, social life, chilling out, me time, time off, commitments, office hours, 9-to-5

work/school | commitments | home life

Commitments: I guess that could be work, school, or home life. Let's put it in the middle.

B Now go to page 148. Do the vocabulary exercises for 8.2.

C GROUP WORK Do you feel you have a busy schedule? Do you get enough downtime? Is your downtime also "me time"?

78

3 GRAMMAR: *I wish*

A Choose the correct words to complete the rules. Use the sentences in the grammar box to help you.

1 *"I wish"* sentences express that you want things to **stay the same / be different**.
2 The main verb of the sentence **stays in the same tense / changes tense**. The modal *"can"* **stays the same / changes to** *could*.
3 Affirmative statements **change to negative / stay affirmative**.
4 Negative statements **change to affirmative / stay negative**.

I wish

I **have to** work long hours.	→	I wish I **didn't have to** work such long hours.
I **don't have** much free time.	→	I wish I **had** more free time.
I **can't take** any time off next week.	→	I wish I **could take** some time off next week.
I **promised** to work this weekend.	→	I wish I **hadn't promised** to work this weekend.

B Now go to page 137. Look at the grammar chart and do the grammar exercise for 8.2.

C PAIR WORK Complete the wishes so that they are true for you. Review them with a partner and check your accuracy.

1 I wish I knew
2 I wish I could
3 I wish I wasn't/weren't
4 I wish I didn't have to
5 I wish I hadn't
6 I wish I had

ACCURACY CHECK

Don't confuse *wish* and *hope*. Use *hope* to talk about something you want to happen in the future.
I hope you'll be there on Saturday.
Use *wish* to talk about a situation you can't change.
I wish you could come on Saturday, but I know you have to work.

4 SPEAKING

A PAIR WORK Look at the list of wishes. Which do you think are the most common? Why?

I wish I had gone to a different college.
I wish I had studied harder in high school.
I wish I could play a musical instrument.
I wish I could get a different job.
I wish I could travel more.
I wish I was younger.
I wish I was older.

B PAIR WORK Think of three more common wishes. Who might have them? Compare your ideas

79

ACCURACY CHECK

Don't confuse *wish* and *hope*. Use *hope* to talk about something you want to happen in the future.

I hope you'll be there on Saturday.

Use *wish* to talk about a situation you can't change.

I wish you could come on Saturday, but I know you have to work.

Accuracy check

INSIGHT

Some common errors can become fossilized if not addressed early on in the learning process.

CONTENT

Accuracy check highlights common learner errors (based on unique research into the Cambridge Learner Corpus) and can be used for self-editing.

RESULT

Students avoid common errors in their written and spoken English.

You spoke. We listened.

Students told us that speaking is the most important skill for them to master, while teachers told us that finding speaking activities which engage their students and work in the classroom can be challenging.

That's why EVOLVE has a whole lesson dedicated to speaking: Lesson 5, *Time to speak*.

Time to speak

INSIGHT

Speaking ability is how students most commonly measure their own progress, but is also the area where they feel most insecure. To be able to fully exploit speaking opportunities in the classroom, students need a safe speaking environment where they can feel confident, supported, and able to experiment with language.

CONTENT

Time to Speak is a unique lesson dedicated to developing speaking skills and is based around immersive tasks which involve information sharing and decision making.

RESULT

Time to speak lessons create a buzz in the classroom where speaking can really thrive, evolve, and take off, resulting in more confident speakers of English.

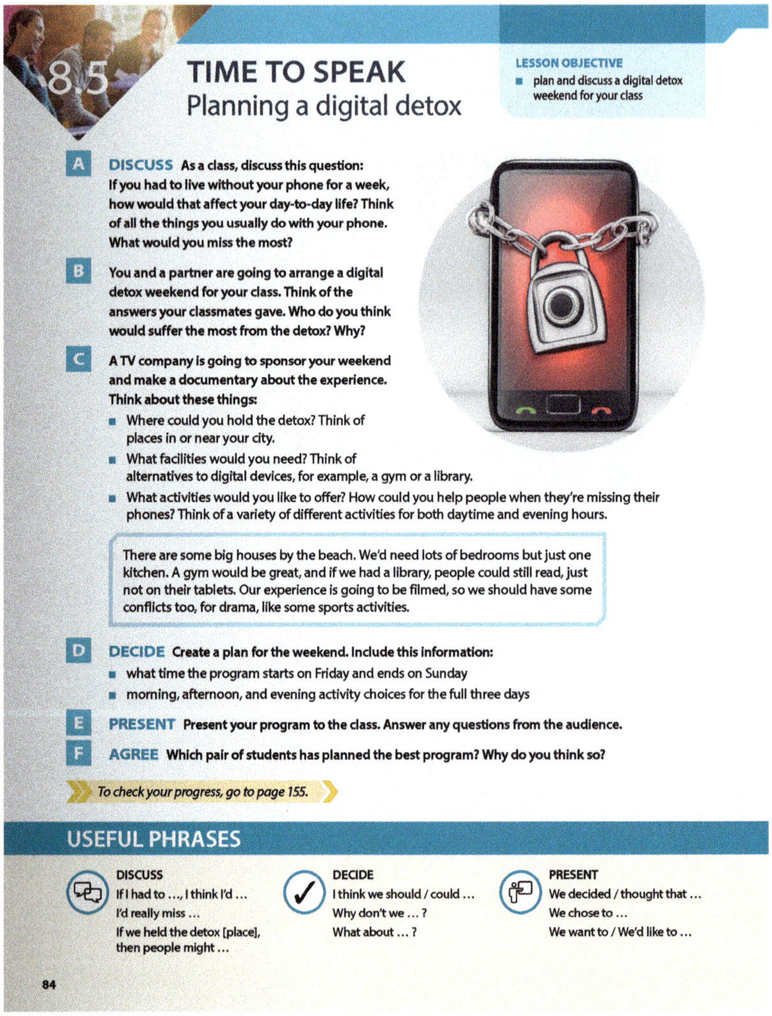

8.5

TIME TO SPEAK
Planning a digital detox

LESSON OBJECTIVE
- plan and discuss a digital detox weekend for your class

A DISCUSS As a class, discuss this question: If you had to live without your phone for a week, how would that affect your day-to-day life? Think of all the things you usually do with your phone. What would you miss the most?

B You and a partner are going to arrange a digital detox weekend for your class. Think of the answers your classmates gave. Who do you think would suffer the most from the detox? Why?

C A TV company is going to sponsor your weekend and make a documentary about the experience. Think about these things:
- Where could you hold the detox? Think of places in or near your city.
- What facilities would you need? Think of alternatives to digital devices, for example, a gym or a library.
- What activities would you like to offer? How could you help people when they're missing their phones? Think of a variety of different activities for both daytime and evening hours.

There are some big houses by the beach. We'd need lots of bedrooms but just one kitchen. A gym would be great, and if we had a library, people could still read, just not on their tablets. Our experience is going to be filmed, so we should have some conflicts too, for drama, like some sports activities.

D DECIDE Create a plan for the weekend. Include this information:
- what time the program starts on Friday and ends on Sunday
- morning, afternoon, and evening activity choices for the full three days

E PRESENT Present your program to the class. Answer any questions from the audience.

F AGREE Which pair of students has planned the best program? Why do you think so?

To check your progress, go to page 155.

USEFUL PHRASES

DISCUSS
If I had to …, I think I'd …
I'd really miss …
If we held the detox [place], then people might …

DECIDE
I think we should / could …
Why don't we … ?
What about … ?

PRESENT
We decided / thought that …
We chose to …
We want to / We'd like to …

84

Experience Better Learning with EVOLVE: a course that helps both teachers and students on every step of the language learning journey.

Speaking matters. Find out more about creating safe speaking environments in the classroom.

EVOLVE unit structure

Unit opening page

Each unit opening page activates prior knowledge and vocabulary and immediately gets students speaking.

Lessons 1 and 2

These lessons present and practice the unit vocabulary and grammar in context, helping students discover language rules for themselves. Students then have the opportunity to use this language in well-scaffolded, personalized speaking tasks.

Lesson 3

This lesson is built around a functional language dialogue that models and contextualizes useful fixed expressions for managing a particular situation. This is a real world strategy to help students handle unexpected conversational turns.

Lesson 4

This is a combined skills lesson based around an engaging reading or listening text. Each lesson asks students to think critically and ends with a practical writing task.

Lesson 5

Time to speak is an entire lesson dedicated to developing speaking skills. Students work on collaborative, immersive tasks which involve information sharing and decision making.

CONTENTS

Functional language	Listening	Reading	Writing	Speaking
■ Meet someone you don't know; introduce someone to others **Real-world strategy** ■ Respond to an introduction		**Flipping your job interview** ■ An article on interview skills	**A comment** ■ A comment on an article ■ Agreeing and disagreeing	■ Talk about a new activity ■ Talk about personal achievements ■ Describe your personal qualities ■ Play an introduction game **Time to speak** ■ Ask and answer interview questions
■ Make, accept, and refuse offers in social situations **Real-world strategy** ■ Acknowledge an acceptance	**Cool food** ■ A conversation between friends		**A report** ■ The results of a survey about eating habits ■ Reporting research results	■ Talk about fusion foods ■ Discuss ideas to avoid food waste ■ Explain a favorite recipe ■ Offer food and drink to others **Time to speak** ■ Present a restaurant rescue plan
■ Make an apology and explain what happened **Real-world strategy** ■ Respond to an apology		**Buyer beware!** ■ Short stories about good and bad online shopping experiences	**A product review** ■ Product reviews ■ Expressing opinions about product features	■ Discuss things money can't buy ■ Talk about quality of life ■ Talk about relative value ■ Talk about a past apology **Time to speak** ■ Repair a customer relationship
■ Exchange and discuss opinions about possible actions **Real-world strategy** ■ Make opinions more emphatic	**Building a brand** ■ A news report about a local company that went global		**A response** ■ A social media post ■ Writing about reasons and consequences	■ Talk about all the signs we see ■ Speculate about a picture ■ Talk about viral stories ■ Give and support opinions **Time to speak** ■ Create and present an ad
■ React to problems and try to find a solution **Real-world strategy** ■ Accepting bad news		**The perfect apology** ■ An article about corporate apologies	**An apology** ■ A letter of apology from a company ■ Using referents to avoid repetition	■ Discuss good storytellers ■ Tell someone's life story ■ Tell the story of a change of plans ■ Act out situations with bad news **Time to speak** ■ Connect events to tell the story
■ Make, refuse, and accept offers of help **Real-world strategy** ■ Imposing on somebody	**Painting safer streets** ■ A podcast about a community art project		**A report** ■ A report on a community project ■ Using quotes as support	■ Talk about acts of kindness ■ Discuss charity organizations ■ Discuss helping others ■ Make offers of help to strangers **Time to speak** ■ Discuss helping your community

CLASSROOM LANGUAGE

PAIR WORK AND GROUP WORK

1.02 Choosing roles

How should we start?

Why don't you be … and I'll be …

Who wants to present for our group?

Understanding the task

So what are we supposed to do?

I'm not really sure.

Should we ask the teacher?

Asking for more time

Sorry, we're not done yet. We need a few more minutes.

Completing a task

OK. So are we done with this part?

I think so. What's next?

TALKING TO THE TEACHER

Discussing assignments

When is … due?

Can I email … to you?

Discussing a missed class

I was out on … Can you tell me what I missed?

Asking for explanations

Can you tell us what we're supposed to do again?

Can you explain that again? I didn't understand.

Preparing for a text/exam

Will this be on the test?

Will we review this before the test?

UNIT OBJECTIVES

- talk about personal achievements
- talk about qualities that employers look for
- make and respond to introductions
- write a comment on a blog post
- practice a job interview

AND WE'RE OFF!

1

START SPEAKING

A Look at the picture. Where is the man? What is he about to do? How do you think he feels? Why?

B PAIR WORK Think of a new activity you are about to start or that you have started recently (a new job, a new sport, a new course, etc.). What is it? How do you feel about it? For ideas, watch Andres's video.

C GROUP WORK Report three things your partner told you to your group.

REAL STUDENT

Do you feel the same as Andres?

1.1 THIS IS ME!

LESSON OBJECTIVE
- talk about personal achievements

1 LANGUAGE IN CONTEXT

A PAIR WORK **Look at the pictures and describe the three people. Then read the blog post, which is a response to a social media challenge, "Five things about me." Which person wrote it? Why do you think that?**

A

B

C

FIVE THINGS ABOUT ME

Here is my answer to the latest blog challenge!
(If I **get 1,000 likes**, my boss will donate $1,000 to charity. So please like my list!)

1. Every year I **set myself a goal** of learning a new skill. I've done a lot of different things. Last year I learned to play chess. This year I've been learning computer animation and design.
2. People tell me I **have a great sense of humor**, and I love to **tell jokes**!
3. A few years ago, while I was working at a summer camp, a girl came screaming out of her cabin because she saw a huge spider on her bed. I hate spiders, but I **faced my fear**, went in there, and caught that spider. I felt so brave! 😉
4. I'm saving money to open a small studio where I can teach art classes. I've always wanted to **run my own business**. I love **working with my hands**, and I want to do something I can really **take pride in**.
5. This year I'm going to **run a marathon**. I don't want to **win a medal** or **break a record** or anything. I just want to finish! I'm sure I can **rise to the challenge**!

2 VOCABULARY: Describing accomplishments

A 1.03 **Read the post again and find the right verb to complete the expressions. Listen and check.**

1	________ pride in something	5	________ to a challenge	9	________ your fear
2	________ a goal for yourself	6	________ a marathon	10	________ a medal
3	________ a sense of humor	7	________ a business	11	________ a record
4	________ with your hands	8	________ a lot of likes	12	________ a joke

B **Now go to page 141. Do the vocabulary exercises for 1.1.**

C PAIR WORK **Complete the sentences as many times as possible using the expressions in exercise A. Then compare your sentences with a partner. How many things do you have in common?**

1 I have never …

2 I would/wouldn't like to …

I have never told a joke in English.

D PAIR WORK **Imagine you are going to do the blog challenge. What five pieces of information would you choose to share?**

3 GRAMMAR: Tense review (simple and continuous)

A **Complete the descriptions of different tenses. Use the sentences in the grammar box to help you.**

Which tense describes …

1 past experiences with no specific past time given? *present perfect*

2 an action in progress in the past? ______

3 a completed action in the past? ______

4 a habit or repeated action in the present? ______

5 an action in progress in the present? ______

6 an action that started sometime in the past and is still continuing? ______

Simple and continuous tenses

simple present	Every year I **set** myself a goal of learning a new skill.
present continuous	I**'m saving** money to open a small studio.
simple past	I **faced** my fear, **went** in there, and **caught** that spider.
past continuous	I **was working** in a summer camp when it happened.
present perfect	I**'ve done** a lot of different things.
present perfect continuous	This year I**'ve been learning** computer animation.

B **Now go to page 129. Look at the grammar chart and do the grammar exercise for 1.1.**

C **Choose five time expressions from the box and write sentences that are true for you.**

at the moment	at 8 o'clock this morning	never	every day
last year	for the last three months	now	once a week
since I was a child	when I got home	yesterday	

It was raining when I left the house this morning.

D GROUP WORK **Read your sentences to your group. How many of your sentences are the same or similar?**

4 SPEAKING

A PAIR WORK **Read the sentences and discuss which ones are true for you. If they are false, explain why.**

1 I won a medal when I was in high school.

2 I've been studying English for more than 10 years.

3 I once got more than 100 likes for a post on social media.

4 I'm saving money to go on vacation next year.

5 I have never been afraid of anything.

B GROUP WORK **Report back to the class on the five things you learned about your partner.**

Juan runs marathons, and he's won five medals for running. He's been studying English for three years. He doesn't like social media, so he's never …

1.2 THE RIGHT CANDIDATE

LESSON OBJECTIVE
- talk about qualities that employers look for

1 LANGUAGE IN CONTEXT

A 1.04 **Look at the picture. Where are the people? What do you think their relationship is? What do you think they're talking about? Listen to their conversation to check your answers.**

B 1.04 **Listen again and read the script. Do you think she'll get the job? Why or why not?**

1.04 Audio script

A She was so nice. She'd be good with customers – **polite**, friendly, relaxed. She had a lot of **enthusiasm** too, really positive about working with us.

B And she seemed pretty **ambitious** too, you know? She wants to be **successful** in her job, and she's looking for a challenge.

A Yeah, and I really like it when candidates show **curiosity** about how things work here. It shows she's **confident**. I mean, she's not afraid to ask questions, to be **truthful** about what she *doesn't* know.

B No paid work **experience**, but she has other **qualifications**.

A Yeah, she's working on that community art project at the moment and really loving it. That shows **creativity**, too.

B Remember when she was talking about working with kids? She said, "I'm being really careful with how I use social media with them." That's great – it shows she's a **responsible** person.

A Totally! And she seemed to be pretty **independent**, too. Like, she doesn't need someone to tell her what to do all the time.

B Yeah. Well, I think we've found the right person for the job.

2 VOCABULARY: Describing key qualities

A 1.05 **Complete the chart with the bold words from the conversation. Listen and check.**

adjective	noun	adjective	noun	adjective	noun
ambitious	ambition	enthusiastic		qualified	
	confidence	experienced			responsibility
creative			independence		success
curious			politeness		truthfulness

B **Now go to page 141. Do the vocabulary exercises for 1.2.**

C PAIR WORK **Match four words from the chart with the definitions below. Then write short definitions for four others. Read them to another pair. Can they guess the word?**

1 belief in your own abilities
2 describing someone who doesn't lie
3 describing someone who can do things on their own
4 the education, training, and experience needed (pl)

D **Which qualities in the chart above do you think are most important for a new employee? A boss? A friend? Why?**

3 GRAMMAR: Dynamic and stative verbs

A **Circle all correct answers to complete the rules. Use the sentences in the grammar box to help you.**

1 Dynamic verbs describe …
   a an action in progress. **b** an opinion. **c** a plan.
   d a personal quality. **e** a preference.

2 Stative verbs describe …
   a an action in progress. **b** an opinion. **c** a plan.
   d a personal quality. **e** a preference.

3 … verbs usually are not used in the continuous form.
   a Dynamic **b** Stative **c** Both dynamic and stative

4 Some verbs, such as *be* and *think*, …
   a are only dynamic. **b** are only stative. **c** can be dynamic and stative.

Dynamic and stative verbs

Dynamic	She's **working** on a community art project.
	She's **thinking** of looking for a new job.
	I'**m being** really careful with how I use social media.
Stative	She **wants** to be successful in her job.
	I **think** she'd be good with customers.
	She'**s** a responsible person.

B **Now go to page 130. Look at the grammar chart and do the grammar exercise for 1.2.**

C PAIR WORK **Look at the verbs in the pairs of sentences. What's the difference in meaning?**

1 **a** I **love** chocolate cake!
   b I'**m loving** this chocolate cake.

2 **a** She **studies** really hard for her exams.
   b She'**s studying** really hard for her exams.

3 **a** I **think** swimming is a great sport.
   b I'**m thinking** of going swimming.

INSIDER ENGLISH

Some stative verbs (*love, like, hate*) can also be dynamic to talk about enjoyment at the moment.

I'm loving it!

4 SPEAKING

A PAIR WORK **Think of job interview questions you could ask to find out if a job applicant has each of the qualities in the box. Then practice asking and answering the questions. What did you find out about your partner's key qualities?**

ambition
creativity
enthusiasm
independence
truthfulness

Do you prefer to work alone or on a big team?

1.3 WE GO WAY BACK

LESSON OBJECTIVE
- make and respond to introductions

1 FUNCTIONAL LANGUAGE

A PAIR WORK **Look at the picture. Where are these people? What is the relationship between the people? What are they saying to each other?**

B 1.06 **Read and listen to two conversations at the party. Which people know each other? Which people are meeting for the first time?**

1.06 Audio script

1	**Rosa**	Hi, **I don't think we've met before. You're new here, right?** I'm Rosa.
	Mike	Hi, Rosa. Nice to meet you. I'm Mike. And yes, I just started today.
	Rosa	So **this is your first day!** Welcome to the company! **Do you know anyone here?**
	Mike	Well, I've met a couple of people, but there are a lot of people I don't know yet.
	Rosa	Ok, **let me introduce you** to some people.
2	**Rosa**	Hey, Ricardo, do you know Mike?
	Ricardo	No, I don't. Hi, Mike. Nice to meet you!
	Mike	Hi, Ricardo. Great to meet you, too.
	Ricardo	Hey, **have you met Pedro?** He studied in Atlanta and then worked there for about six years. Pedro, come over here!
	Pedro	What's up? Hi, Mike! How are you settling in?
	Mike	Hey, Pedro. Great thanks.
	Rosa	**Do you two know each other?**
	Mike	Yeah, Pedro was the first person I met this morning.

C **Complete the chart with the bold expressions from the conversations.**

Meeting someone for the first time	Introducing someone to a coworker or friend
I don't think we've [1] ________ before.	Do you [3] ________ anyone here?
You're [2] ________ here, right?	Let me [4] ________ you to some people.
Is this your first day?	Have you [5] ________ Pedro?
	Do you two [6] ________ each other?

D 1.07 PAIR WORK **Complete the conversation with expressions from the chart, and check your accuracy. Listen and check. Then practice it with a partner.**

A Hi, I'm Dana. I don't think [1] ________________ .
B No, we haven't. Nice to meet you, Dana, I'm Steve.
A Hi, Steve. You're [2] ________________ , right?
B Yes, that's right. It's my [3] ________________ .
A Hey, welcome! Let me [4] ________________
________________ .

ACCURACY CHECK

Use *meet* for introductions. Use *know* for an ongoing relationship.

Nice to ~~know~~ you. ✗
Nice to meet you. ✓
Do you two know each other? ✓

2 REAL-WORLD STRATEGY

A 1.08 **Listen to two introductions. Do the people already know each other?**

RESPONDING TO AN INTRODUCTION

When someone is introducing you to another person, they usually start by asking, *Have you met / Do you know* [name]*?* You can respond with these expressions.

Yes, we met this morning! Nice to see you again.

Yeah, we go way back. How's it going?

I'm not sure, but hi, I'm …

No, I haven't / don't. Hi, I'm …

B 1.08 **Read the information in the box above. Listen again and complete the conversations.**

1 **A** Do you two know each other?
B Sure do!
C ______
A Really? I had no idea.

2 **A** Have you met Chris?
B ______
C Hi, Toni. Good to meet you.

C GROUP WORK **Work in groups of three. Student A asks Student B if they know Student C. Student B decides which answer to give. Students A and C react appropriately.**

3 PRONUNCIATION FOCUS: Saying the letter *y*

A 1.09 **Listen and repeat. Focus on the letter *y*.**

1 Hi **Y**olanda.
2 Have **y**ou met Ricardo **y**et?

B 1.10 **Listen. Who says the letter *y*? Write A or B.**

1 Yolanda ___ 3 yet ___ 5 yeah ___
2 you ___ 4 year ___ 6 yellow ___

C PAIR WORK **Say the words in exercise 3B to your partner. Does your partner say the letter *y* clearly?**

4 SPEAKING

A PAIR WORK **You are at a party together. Student B is a famous person (decide who together). Student A introduces Student B to the class with only a first name. The class greets Student B and asks questions until they figure out who he or she is.**

Hi, this is Maite.

Hi, Maite, nice to meet you. Your face looks familiar. Are you an actor?

1.4 FLIPPING YOUR JOB INTERVIEW

LESSON OBJECTIVE

- write a comment on a blog post

1 READING

A **PREDICT** **Look at the picture. What are the people waiting for? How are they feeling?**

B **READ FOR GIST** **Read the article from a job search site. Match each heading to the correct section in the article and write it there.**

Questions = Answers The big day A two-way street

Flipping your job interview

A ______

Finally! You've landed an interview for a great job. You've done your homework, prepared answers for all the usual questions, done your research on the company, its products, and its customers. There's nothing left to do but cross your fingers and hope. Or is there?

B ______

A job interview is not a one-way conversation. The company is looking for the right candidate, but you're also looking for something – the right job for you.

Come prepared with a few questions that show you are serious about the job. Think about how you want to develop your skills, your training interests, the types of projects you'd like to work on. You can also ask about the social side, if it's a fun place to work – though maybe not in so many words!

C ______

Your answers to their questions are important, but the questions you ask will also help you make a good impression. If you ask about training opportunities, they know you want to learn. If you ask about career paths, they know you have long-term goals. If you ask your interviewer about their own career, they know you are a person who respects their coworkers.

Flip the interview! Be confident and ask the questions that will help you decide if this is the job for you.

C **Read the article again. Choose the best summary.**

a The article recommends different ways to impress an interviewer.

b The article suggests a different way to prepare for a job interview.

c The article explains what happens after a job interview.

D **INFER MEANING** **Explain the meaning of the bold phrases.**

1 You've **landed an interview** for a great job.

2 You've **done your homework**, prepared answers for all the usual questions …

3 There's nothing left to do but **cross your fingers** and hope.

E **GROUP WORK** **THINK CRITICALLY** **Do you agree with the ideas in the article? Do you think this is a good approach in all job interview situations? Why or why not?**

I'm not sure this is good advice because …

I disagree. I think this is good advice because …

2 WRITING

A **Read the comments on the article. Which one is …**

1 asking for more information? ____
2 disagreeing? ____
3 agreeing? ____

Comments

Share Like Comment

A 

I'm sorry, but I think you're being a bit unrealistic. In today's job market, not all jobs are going to be the perfect job. I think it could have a negative effect if you ask too many questions. And what if your questions tell the interviewer that you're NOT right for the job? You could hurt yourself rather than help yourself!

2 13 2

B 

Thank you for the really useful information. Can you help me with one thing? I'm not too clear on how best to phrase the questions you suggest. I don't want look like I'm interviewing them, but I do want to show them that I am a strong, focused, career-minded person. Your help would be great. Thanks!

1 4 5

C 

I'm a career counselor with an employment agency. I interview clients all day long and find possible jobs for them. Then they interview for the job with the company. The advice you give in this article is completely right. Companies love it when candidates have good questions and aren't afraid to ask them. It really shows them that you are serious about your career and the company.

4 20 8

B WRITING SKILL **Read the comments again. Find phrases used for the following purposes.**

1 to agree: ____
2 to disagree: ____
3 to show appreciation: ____

WRITE IT

C **Write your own comment in response to the article. Use appropriate phrases for agreeing, disagreeing, and/or showing appreciation. Write 50–75 words.**

D GROUP WORK **Share your comment with your group. Do you agree with each other's comments? Why or why not?**

REGISTER CHECK

In both formal and informal writing, use phrases like *a bit* and *a little* to soften a negative comment or opinion.

1.5 TIME TO SPEAK
Job interviews

LESSON OBJECTIVE
- practice a job interview

FIND IT

A **PREPARE** **Read the ad for a tour guide or use your phone to find another ad. What do you think are the main requirements for the job in each of the categories? Make notes.**

education | experience
personal qualities | skills

Tour Guide, full-time

We are looking for a local guide to work with international visitors at our hotel. You will be responsible for organizing short walking and bus tours around the main places of interest in the town as well as offering advice on restaurants, shopping, local events, etc.

B **Work in two groups.**

Group A: You work for the employer. Decide on the questions to ask the candidates.

Group B: You have applied for the job. Prepare yourself for the interview (come up with any qualifications and experience you want) and think about questions you can ask about the job and the company.

C **PRESENT** **Each student from Group A interviews a candidate from Group B.**

Student A: Take notes on the answers given by Student B.

Student B: Make a note of any information you get about the job and the company.

D **AGREE** **Work again with your original group from exercise B.**

Group A: Report back on the various candidates and choose the best candidate.

Group B: Report back on the various companies and choose the best employer.

E **Share your decisions with the class and explain your choices.**

To check your progress, go to page 153.

USEFUL PHRASES

PREPARE

A college degree probably isn't necessary, but …

A tour guide needs to be friendly, organized, …

Previous experience would be …

PRESENT

Why do you want to be a … ?

Do you have any previous experience?

In the past, I have …

AGREE

I think … is the best candidate. She studied history, …

… would be a good employer because …

I wouldn't want to work for … because …

2 THE FUTURE OF FOOD

UNIT OBJECTIVES

- talk about trends
- talk about preparing food
- make, accept, and refuse offers in social situations
- write the results of a survey
- create a plan to improve a restaurant

START SPEAKING

A **Look at the picture. What would you call this dish? What ingredients does it have? What ingredients does this type of food usually have? Would you like to try it? Why or why not?**

B **The dish is an example of a "fusion food": a mixture of different types of foods. What fusion foods do you know about? Have you tried any of them? Describe them. For ideas, watch Maryne's video.**

REAL STUDENT

Do you know about this food?

2.1 MENU WITH A MISSION

LESSON OBJECTIVE
- talk about trends

1 LANGUAGE IN CONTEXT

A **Read the online article about chef Dan Barber. Which statement best summarizes Barber's ideas?**

a People shouldn't waste so much food. **b** People should only cook and eat vegetables.

Would you order a "Dumpster Dive Vegetable Salad"? Would you eat food that other people throw away? Dan Barber is a respected chef, and he is offering his customers just that. For Barber, luxury ingredients are **a thing of the past**. His restaurants make the most of ingredients that are far from **fashionable.** Some would even call them trash. Barber doesn't care what food looks like, "if it tastes good, eat it!" So, if you prefer good flavor to good looks, you'll love his food.

Restaurants always offer a doggy bag if you want to take food home, but Barber takes it a step further and promotes "zero waste." And this isn't just a **fad**. The idea is **gaining popularity** in the restaurant world.

Barber's restaurants are among the **trendiest** in the U.S., which surprises me. Can his unusual dishes really be good? But I might agree to try something if a professional chef like Barber serves it – even those ugly carrots!

GLOSSARY

dumpster (*n*) large metal container into which people put waste

doggy bag (*n*) a small container to take home unfinished food

2 VOCABULARY: Describing trends

A 1.11 PAIR WORK **Look at the expressions in the box. Listen and say the words. Are they talking about an upward trend, a downward trend, or a description of something's popularity? Think of examples to support your answers.**

be a fad	be a thing of the past	be all the rage	be fashionable
be old-fashioned	be on the way out	be the latest thing	be the next big thing
be trendy	come back in style	gain interest	gain popularity
go out of style	lose interest	lose popularity	

A fad is something that is popular for a short time, so that's a description of popularity.

Yeah, fidget spinners are a recent fad.

B **Now go to page 142. Do the vocabulary exercises for 2.1.**

C GROUP WORK **Think of other trends and fashions. Complete the sentences so that they are true in your opinion and explain why. You can use your phone to find interesting images to support your opinion.**

FIND IT

1 For men, beards are definitely …
2 A trend I really like is …
3 … is definitely going out of style.
4 Some old-fashioned things are nice. I hope … come(s) back in style.

INSIDER ENGLISH

Use *be trending* to talk about a topic or issue that is very popular at the moment.

Gray hair for young women ***is trending*** *on social media.*

3 GRAMMAR: Real conditionals

A **Choose the correct option to complete the rules. Use the sentences in the grammar box to help you. (Remember that either clause can come first in a conditional sentence.)**

1 Use *if* + present, present to …
   a talk about future results. **b** tell someone what to do. **c** talk about things that are generally true.

2 Use *if* + present, *will / be going to / might* to …
   a talk about future results. **b** tell someone what to do. **c** talk about things that are generally true.

3 Use *if* + present, imperative to …
   a talk about future results. **b** tell someone what to do. **c** talk about things that are generally true.

Real conditionals

Restaurants offer a doggy bag if you want to take food home.
If you **prefer** good flavor to good looks, you**'ll** love his food.
I **might** agree to try something **if** Barber **serves** it.
If it **tastes** good, **eat** it!

B **Now go to page 130. Look at the grammar chart and do the grammar exercise for 2.1.**

C PAIR WORK **Rewrite the sentences as real conditionals. Then check your accuracy.**

1 Vegetarians don't eat meat.
   If you are a vegetarian, you don't eat meat.
2 You like Italian food, so it is possible that Tito's is a good restaurant for you to try.
3 Do you like fish? Yes? Then I think Japanese food is a great choice for you.
4 Here are some cookies. You have my permission to eat them.

✓ ACCURACY CHECK

Never use *will* or *might* in an *if* clause.

If I ~~won't/might not~~ eat, I'll be hungry. ✗
If I don't eat, I'll be hungry. ✓

D PAIR WORK **Complete the sentences about restaurants and eating out in your area. Discuss your ideas with your partner.**

1 If you want to try something new or different …
2 If you want really healthy food …
3 If you want to try a trendy restaurant downtown …

4 SPEAKING

A GROUP WORK **Which foods do you sometimes have to throw out? Why?**

I often throw out fruit because I buy too much and can't eat it before it goes bad.

B **Give each other advice about using that food. Then share your ideas with the class. Who has the best idea?**

If you have old fruit, make a smoothie!

2.2 FOOD YOU FERMENT

LESSON OBJECTIVE
- talk about preparing food

1 VOCABULARY: Preparing food

A 1.12 PAIR WORK **Listen and say the words. Then decide what type of food each item is: fish/seafood, vegetable, herb/spice, or fruit. Which foods do you like or dislike? Why?**

B 1.13 PAIR WORK **Look at the verbs for preparing food. Listen and say the words. Which foods can you prepare in this way?**

barbecue

boil

chop

fry

rinse

stir

You should rinse fruits and vegetables before eating them.

A ______

B ______

C ______

D ______

E ______

F ______

G ______

H ______

I ______

C **Now go to page 142. Do the vocabulary exercises for 2.2.**

2 LANGUAGE IN CONTEXT

A 1.14 **Look at the pictures at the top of the next page. What dish do you think it is? Where do you think it comes from? Does it look easy or difficult to make? Listen to the podcast and check your answers.**

1.14 Audio script

Today we're going to prepare *kimchi*, a spicy cabbage recipe from Korea. Even if you don't like cabbage, after you hear this recipe, you'll want to try it. Let's begin!

First, **chop** a head of cabbage into small pieces, cover it with salt, and leave it in water. Let it stand for about two hours, then **rinse** the cabbage in cold water and drain it. **Stir** together the garlic, ginger, and sugar. Add in shrimp paste and a chili powder called *gochugaru*. Then add in the spring onions and radish. Use your hands to mix it all together with the cabbage – remember to wear gloves!

Finally, put the kimchi into a jar and leave it to ferment. You'll have to wait about five days until the kimchi is ready to eat. When the flavor is just right, transfer it to the fridge – that stops the fermentation process.

Kimchi will stay fresh in the fridge for up to three months. Your guests will be so impressed when they try it. You'll see!!

B 1.14 **Listen again. Put the images in the correct order and summarize each step of the recipe. Is this a dish that you would like to eat, or try to make?**

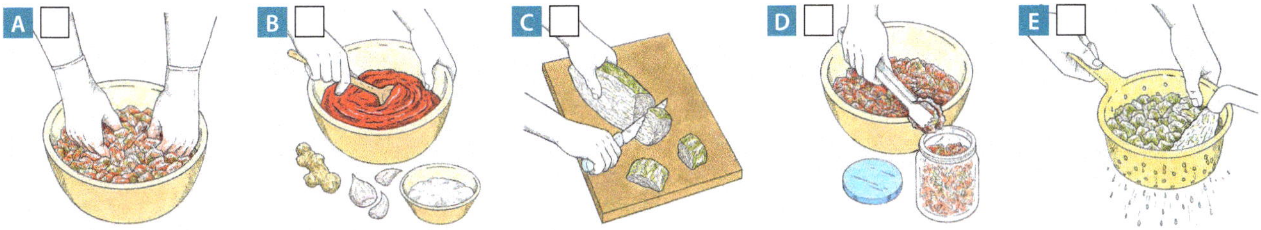

3 GRAMMAR: Clauses with *after, until, when*

A **Complete the rules. Use the sentences in the grammar box to help you.**

To talk about a sequence of events in the future …

1 use a time clause with *after, until, when* + **present** / **future** tense.

2 keep the main clause of the sentence in **present** / **future** tense.

Clauses with *after, until, when*

After you hear the recipe, you'll want to try it.
Your guests will be so impressed **when** they try it.
You'll have to wait about five days **until** the kimchi is ready to eat.

! **You can use many other time expressions with this structure: *as soon as, before, once …***

*Your guests will love it **once** they try it!*

B **Write the verb in parentheses ( ) in the correct tense.**

1 After you ______ (bake) the cake, I ______ (come) over and decorate it with you.
2 Until I ______ (see) it for myself, I ______ (not believe) it.
3 Once she ______ (finish) school, she ______ (travel) in South America.
4 They ______ (join) us at the restaurant as soon as the concert ______ (be) over.
5 He ______ (give) you the recipe when he ______ (see) you next week.

C **Now go to page 131. Do the grammar exercise for 2.2.**

D PAIR WORK **Answer the questions so that they are true for you. Compare your answers with your partner.**

- What's the first thing you're going to do when you get home tonight?
- Is there anything you need to do before you go home today?

4 SPEAKING

A PAIR WORK **What are some typical dishes in your country or region? Are they easy or difficult to make?**

Gazpacho is a typical dish. It's delicious and not difficult to make.

FIND IT

B PAIR WORK **Describe a dish that you like and explain how to prepare it. You can find images on your phone to help you explain. For ideas, watch Maryne's video.**

Would you like to try the dish Maryne described?

2.3 CAN I GET YOU A REFILL?

LESSON OBJECTIVE

- make, accept, and refuse offers in social situations

1 FUNCTIONAL LANGUAGE

A PAIR WORK 1.15 **Look at the photo. Discuss the questions. Read and listen to the conversation. Were you correct?**

1 What kind of food are the people having?
2 What other things do you think they will serve?
3 Is it a formal or an informal occasion?

1.15 Audio script

A **Can I get you** anything else to drink?
B Oh, yes. Can I have a soda, please?
A **Would you like** a regular one?
B Do you have sugarless ones?
A Sure, **here you go.** One diet soda.
B **Thanks, that's great.**
A No worries. **Anybody else want** a hotdog before I, um, burn them?
C Me, please!
A Coming right up! There's also dessert in the kitchen, you know, when you're ready for it. It's buffet style, so **help yourself**.
C **Awesome, I'll check it out** later. Great barbecue!
A Thanks. Oh, Grace, would you **care for a refill**?
D **No, I'm good. Thanks anyway.**
A **Can I offer you another** hotdog then?
D **That'd be wonderful.**
A You got it. Hey, there are plenty of hotdogs here. Anybody want seconds? Jason?
E **I better not**. I've already had thirds!

B **Complete the chart with the bold expressions from the conversation.**

Making offers	Accepting offers	Refusing offers
Can I get / offer you (something to drink)? [1] ______ you like / care for (a refill)? [2] ______ /There you go. Anybody else want (a hotdog)? [3] ______ yourself!	[4] ______, that's great. Awesome, I'll [5] ______ it out. That'd be wonderful.	No, I'm [6] ______ . No, but thanks anyway. I better not.

C 1.16 PAIR WORK **Complete the conversations with the expressions from the chart. Listen and check. Practice the conversations with a partner. Then change the offers and the responses. Use your own ideas.**

1 A [1] ______ I get you a refill?
B That'd be wonderful. I really need caffeine this morning!
A [2] ______ you go.
B Mm, thanks!

2 A Would you [3] ______ for more cake?
B No, I'm [4] ______ . I'm really full!
A Can I [5] ______ you more iced tea then?
B Yes! That'd be great!

2 REAL-WORLD STRATEGY

A 1.17 **Listen to part of the conversation again. What does the host say when people accept his offers?**

ACKNOWLEDGE AN ACCEPTANCE

When someone accepts your offer of food or drink, it's polite to acknowledge it.

You got it!

Coming right up! *One sec.*

I'll be right back with that. *Sure thing.*

B 1.18 **Read about acknowledging acceptance in the box above. Use the expressions there to complete the conversation below. Then listen and check.**

! *sec = second*

Attendant Hello. Can I get you something to drink, ma'am?

Customer Yes, hot tea, please.

Attendant [1] ________________ . Sugar?

Customer Yes, thanks. And could I have some milk for it, too?

Attendant [2] ________________ . I'll get some from the fridge. I'll be [3] ________________ .

C PAIR WORK **Student A: You are the flight attendant. Make two offers to the customer and acknowledge their responses. Student B: You are the customer. Accept one offer and reject the other. Change roles and do the conversation again.**

3 PRONUNCIATION FOCUS: Saying the vowel sounds /aɪ/, /i/, and /eɪ/

A 1.19 **Listen and repeat the three different vowel sounds.**

/aɪ/ like	/i/ please	/eɪ/ great
Would you **like** a regular one?	Can I have a soda, **please**?	That's **great**.

B 1.20 **Listen. Write A for words with /aɪ/. Write B for words with /i/. Write C for words with /eɪ/.**

1 Grace ____ 3 Jason ____ 5 caffeine ____

2 style ____ 4 refill ____ 6 iced tea ____

C 1.21 PAIR WORK **Listen to the conversations. Then practice with a partner.**

1 A Would you like a refill?
B Yes, please. That'd be great.

2 A Could I have another slice of cake?
B Coming right up!

4 SPEAKING

A PAIR WORK **Student A: You're hosting a few friends at home. Student B: You're a guest. Practice making and responding to offers involving food and drink. Then switch roles and do it again.**

Can I get you something other than water with your meal? A soda maybe?

No. I'm good with water. I'm watching my weight.

Are you sure? I have diet soda.

Oh, then yes, that'd be great.

2.4 COOL FOOD

LESSON OBJECTIVE
- write the results of a survey

1 LISTENING

A 1.22 LISTEN FOR GIST **Look at the pictures. What attitudes about food do you think they represent? Listen to a conversation between two friends and check your answers. Were you right?**

B 1.22 LISTEN FOR DETAILS **Listen again and answer the questions.**

1 What are Ricardo's objections to coconut water?
2 What reasons does Anna give for drinking it?
3 What does Ricardo say about gluten-free products?
4 Does Anna agree with him?

C PAIR WORK CRITICAL THINKING **Food packaging and labels provide information about the food we eat. Discuss the questions.**

- Do you read the information on food packaging? Do you think the information is important? Do you think it is accurate? Does it influence your food shopping decisions? Why or why not?
- How often do you try new foods or brands of food? How much do you think the packaging increases your curiosity about a new food item? Think of a time when you tried something just because you liked the packaging or label. What was it? Were you pleased or disappointed?
- What other information about food do you think is important to know? Should that information be on the packaging, too? Why or why not?

2 PRONUNCIATION: Listening for deleted /t/ sounds

A 1.23 **Listen to each sentence. Focus on the bold word. Do you hear the /t/ sound?**

	Yes	No
1 Do you **want** me to get you a coconut water?	☐	☐
2 Sure, I **trust** the experts …	☐	☐
3 I guess you've **got** a point …	☐	☐
4 The **latest** thing is eating gluten free …	☐	☐

B **Choose the correct word to complete the sentence.**

Final /t/ sounds are often deleted when they are followed by a *consonant* / *vowel*.

3 WRITING

A **As part of an economics course, some students conducted a survey about attitudes towards food. Read the results. Do the results surprise you? Why or why not?**

Changing food habits

Worldwide the food industry (including both growing and selling food) is estimated to be worth 4.8 trillion dollars every year. That makes it the world's largest industry. It also means that understanding people's attitudes about what they eat is very important. We recently conducted a survey of people's attitudes toward certain food trends.

Our survey shows that attitudes to health food trends are much more positive in Latin America than in the U.S. and Canada. In Latin America, a little over half of those we surveyed were willing to pay more for all natural foods. In the U.S. / Canada, the number was less than 25%. Similarly, 31% of people interviewed from Latin America said they would pay more for gluten-free products. But in the U.S. / Canada, 10% fewer people reported that they would pay more for gluten-free foods.

These trends can also be seen in food sales in both regions. In Latin America, sales of "healthy" foods grew 16% in a two-year period. In the U.S. / Canada, the growth in sales was less than 10%.

REGISTER CHECK

Using the passive voice can give your writing a more academic tone.

You can also see these trends in food sales in both regions. (informal, non-academic)

These trends can also be seen in food sales in both regions. (formal, academic)

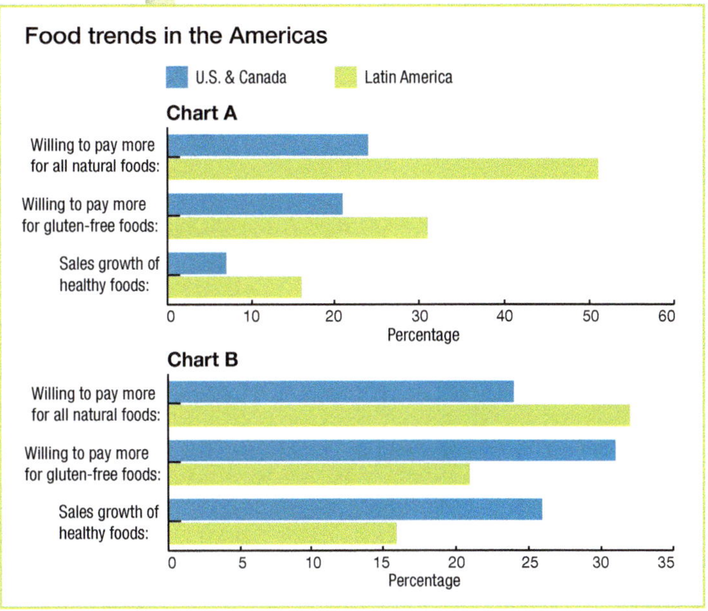

B **Look again at the survey results. Which chart matches the information?**

C WRITING SKILL **Complete the phrases used for giving results.**

1 Our survey ________________ that …

2 In Latin America, a little over half ________________ said …

3 31% ________________ from Latin America …

4 But in the U.S. / Canada, 10% fewer ________________ they …

D GROUP WORK **Work together to write 3–5 survey questions about some aspect of changing eating habits. Then conduct your survey individually.**

Our survey is about meal times. Question 1: What time did you eat breakfast when you were a child, and when do you eat breakfast now?

WRITE IT

E **Come back together and share results within your group. Work together to write the results of your survey. Write about 130 words. Make a chart to illustrate your results.**

Our survey shows that meal times … . As you can see in the chart, 25% of those we interviewed reported that they eat breakfast …

F **Share your group's survey topic and results with the class. Which group's results were particularly surprising or interesting to you?**

2.5 TIME TO SPEAK
Rescue the restaurant!

LESSON OBJECTIVE
- create a plan to improve a restaurant

A Look at the picture. Do you think the restaurant is successful? Why or why not?

B **RESEARCH** Divide into two groups, Group A and Group B. Group A: Read about Chow Mein Tacos on page 157. Group B: Read about Veggie Heaven on page 159. Identify the problems and make notes.

C **PREPARE** Divide each group into teams of three or four. As a team, think of possible solutions to the problems you identified in your restaurant. Then use your ideas to create an action plan for the restaurant owners. Some ideas to consider in your plan:

acoustics (sound quality and volume)
atmosphere (decoration, lighting, music)
client profile
ingredients
marketing
menu
premises
special offers

D **PRESENT** Present your team's plan to your group. Which ideas are the best or most original? Why? Combine the best ideas from all the teams into one action plan. Then present your restaurant, its main problems, and your action plan to the class.

E **AGREE** Which group has the better plan for improvement? Do you think it's possible to save either or both restaurants? Why or why not?

To check your progress, go to page 153.

USEFUL PHRASES

RESEARCH
To me, the biggest problem is …
They could solve this by …
If they only serve …, more people will …

PREPARE
To improve …, they could …
If they …, customers will …
They could try …

PRESENT
We suggest three main changes: …
If this restaurant wants to stay open, it'll have to …
After they redecorate, they'll need to …

UNIT OBJECTIVES

- discuss the relative importance of time and money
- discuss value and how we measure it
- apologize for damaging or losing someone else's property
- write a product review
- discuss ways to respond to a negative product review

WHAT'S IT WORTH?

3

START SPEAKING

A **Look at the poster. Where would you expect to see it? Do you agree with the message? Why or why not?**

B **Write a list of five things money can't buy. Then write your own version of the message and share it with the class. For ideas, watch Andres's video. Whose version do you most agree with?**

REAL STUDENT

Do you agree with Andres?

3.1 IS IT WORTH IT?

LESSON OBJECTIVE

- discuss the relative importance of time and money

1 LANGUAGE IN CONTEXT

A 1.24 **What is more important to you? Time or money? Why? Listen to a podcast interview with two young professionals. Which do they feel is more important? What are their reasons?**

1.24 Audio script

Host Time and money. Two things most people don't have enough of. With the [a] **cost of living** going up and long commutes, is it possible to find a good [b] **balance**? Sue Mendez hated the hour-long commute to work. Last fall, she took a new job in her neighborhood, but she also [c] **took a salary cut.**

Sue I was spending too much time on a bus. I'm glad I [d] **traded** my old job for my new [e] **lifestyle.** I had to move to a smaller apartment, but it [f] **was worth it.** I make enough money to get by, and I really [g] **value** all my free time!

Host Dirk Monroe, on the other hand, [h] **can't afford** a salary cut. He has a family and needs the money. He spends his hour-long commute listening to music.

Dirk I don't mind it. It's [i] **time well spent.** It's just long enough to help me relax after work. And I'm not too tired to play with the kids when I get home.

Host What about you, which do you value more? Money, to [j] **boost** your [k] **standard of living**, or time, to improve your [l] **quality of life**?

2 VOCABULARY: Talking about time and money

A 1.25 **Match the bold words and phrases in the podcast with the definitions below. Listen and check.**

1 exchange one thing for another (verb) *d*
2 a good use of time (phrase) ___
3 general level of happiness (phrase) ___
4 equal importance (noun and verb) ___
5 how much we have to pay for our basic needs (phrase) ___
6 make something bigger (verb) ___
7 ability to meet basic needs (phrase) ___
8 not have enough money to do or buy something (phrase) ___
9 the way you live (noun) ___
10 get less money for your work (phrase) ___
11 have a positive result (phrase) ___
12 feel the importance of (noun and verb) ___

B **Now go to page 143. Do the vocabulary exercises for 3.1.**

C PAIR WORK **What activities do you spend the most time on every week? Which ones do you think are time well spent? Which are a waste of time? Why?**

3 GRAMMAR: *too* and *enough*

A **Choose the correct words to complete the rules. Use the sentences in the grammar box to help you.**

Use (*not*) *too* and (*not*) *enough* with adjectives and nouns to say if a situation is acceptable or unacceptable.

1 *Too* and *not enough* tell us that something is **acceptable / unacceptable**.

2 *Not too* and *enough* tell us that something is **acceptable / unacceptable**.

3 Phrases with *too* and *enough* are often followed by ***to* + verb / verb**.

too* and *enough

Most people do**n't** have **enough** time.
I was spending **too much** time on a bus.
My commute is just long **enough** to help me relax.
I'm **not too** tired to play with the kids when I get home.

B **Now go to page 131. Look at the grammar chart and do the grammar exercise for 3.1.**

C **Change the sentences in the grammar box to make statements that are true for you. Write four sentences. Check your accuracy.**

I just don't have enough time to go to the grocery store.

D PAIR WORK **Read your sentences to your partner. Are any of your sentences the same?**

✓ **ACCURACY** CHECK

Remember, *enough* comes <u>after</u> an adjective but <u>before</u> a noun.

That's ~~enough good~~ for me. ✗
That's good enough for me. ✓
That's ~~pizza enough~~ for me! ✗
That's enough pizza for me! ✓

4 SPEAKING

A GROUP WORK **Discuss the questions.**

1 What do you think are the most important factors in having a good quality of life? Look at the ideas in the box to help you.

things to do in your free time	a group of close friends	a job you feel proud of
living near your family	access to education	a good salary
time to do the things you want to do		

2 Which do you think is the biggest problem for a good quality of life: time, money, or something different?

3.2 THE PRICE OF COFFEE

LESSON OBJECTIVE
- discuss value and how we measure it

1 LANGUAGE IN CONTEXT

A **How often do you go to cafés? What do you order to drink there? How much does it cost? Do you think it's a good price? Why or why not? Read the review of a coffee shop. What makes it different from other coffee shops?**

A coffee shop with a difference

I just treated myself to by far the best coffee I've ever had, and it was nowhere near as expensive as my usual coffee shop! There's nothing special about the café, though it is a little busier than other places. There's really just one thing that makes it different: You pay what you want.

Every café comes up with its own price to charge for a cup of coffee. It can be much cheaper than other places or a whole lot more expensive, depending on the café's own costs but also things people are willing to pay more for, like atmosphere. If there's a beautiful view, a café makes the most of it with big windows and raises the price a penny. If customers want to take advantage of the free Wi-fi, there's another penny. It all has an effect on the price.

This café, however, suggests a price for its coffee, but most people pay more. They know they can rely on the quality of the coffee, and they like that the café trusts them to pay a fair price for it. They feel they play an important role in the business. And when customers feel invested in your success, how can you lose?

B **Read the review again. Does the reviewer like the café? Do other customers like it? How do you know? Have you ever been to a café or restaurant where you can pay what you want?**

> **!** A *penny* is a coin worth 1/100th of a U.S. dollar. It is often used to represent any small amount of money.

2 VOCABULARY: Talking about prices and value

A 1.26 **Find the expressions in the text and complete them with the correct preposition. Listen and check.**

1 treat yourself ________
2 come up ________
3 charge ________
4 depend ________
5 make the most ________
6 take advantage ________
7 have an effect ________
8 suggest a price ________
9 rely ________
10 pay a fair price ________
11 play an important role ________
12 invest ________

B **Now go to page 143. Do the vocabulary exercises for 3.2.**

C PAIR WORK **Discuss the questions.**

1 Where do you go when you want to treat yourself to a special meal? Does that place charge a fair price for their meals? How much would you pay if you could come up with your own price?
2 Do you think it's a good idea for businesses to suggest a price rather than charge for things? Why or why not?

> *I like to treat myself to dessert at a little café near the station. They charge a lot for some things, but it's worth it!*

3 GRAMMAR: Modifying comparisons

A **Circle the correct answer to complete the rules. Use the sentences in the grammar box to help you.**

1 To show a small difference using comparative adjectives, use ***a little* or *a bit* / *a whole lot* or *much*.**

2 To show a big difference using comparative adjectives, use ***a little* or *a bit* / *a whole lot* or *much*.**

3 To show a small difference using an *as … as …* comparison, use ***nowhere near* / *almost* or *nearly*.**

4 To show a big difference using an *as … as …* comparison, use ***nowhere near* / *almost* or *nearly*.**

5 To show a big difference using superlative adjectives, use ***nowhere near* / *by far*.**

Modifying comparisons

I just treated myself to **by far the best** coffee I've ever had.
It was **nowhere near as expensive as** my usual coffee shop.
It's **a little busier** than other places.
The price can be **much cheaper** or **a whole lot more expensive**.

B **Now go to page 132. Look at the grammar chart and do the grammar exercise for 3.2.**

C PAIR WORK **Compare products and services using the adjectives in the boxes. Make at least three comparisons for each item.**

cheap expensive delicious

1 a burger from a fast-food restaurant / a burger from a local restaurant / a gourmet burger at a five-star restaurant

A burger from a fast-food place is much cheaper than a gourmet burger. A gourmet burger may be a whole lot more expensive, but it is by far the most delicious of the three.

cheap comfortable expensive fashionable

2 some sandals to wear on the beach / a pair of sneakers you bought at the mall / a pair of shoes you bought to go to a wedding

cheap exciting expensive long

3 a bus tour around your city / a train trip to your favorite city / a flight to another country

4 SPEAKING

FIND IT

A GROUP WORK **Look at the products in the box. Put them in order according to how much money you'd be willing to pay for each. Then compare your lists with another group and explain your ideas. You can look up examples on your phone to help support your answer.**

a birthday present
a new phone
a pair of sunglasses
a bottle of perfume/cologne
a pair of jeans

I don't really care about clothes, so I wouldn't spend more than $50 on a pair of jeans. I'd spend a lot more on a nice pair of sunglasses!

3.3 I'M SO SORRY!

LESSON OBJECTIVE
- apologize for damaging or losing someone else's property

1 FUNCTIONAL LANGUAGE

A **Look at the picture. What happened? How would you feel if this happened to you?**

B **1.27 Listen to Justin telling Kathy what happened. How does Kathy react? Why?**

1.27 Audio script

A **I'm really sorry**, but **I just did the dumbest thing.**
B What? What did you do?
A Well, you let me borrow your bike, remember?
B Yeah, I remember.
A Well, I left it outside a store, but only for, like, five minutes!
B Oh no, don't tell me somebody stole it!
A Well, not the whole bike ... just the front tire.
B You mean you didn't lock the front tire?
A I know, Kathy, I know, **I can't believe I didn't lock it. I can't tell you how sorry I am!** I'll go out today and get you another one. I am so, so sorry.
B It's OK, Justin. It's not the end of the world. A new front tire shouldn't cost too much. How about I order one and let you know how much it is?
A Yes, yes, whatever you want. I'll pick it up from the bike store, too.
B OK, deal!

C **Complete the chart with the bold expressions from the conversation.**

Apologizing	Explaining what happened
I'm really sorry. I [1] ________ how sorry I am.	You'll never guess what I did. I just did the [2] ________ thing. I can't [3] ________ I (didn't lock it).

INSIDER ENGLISH

Use "*Oh no, don't tell me*" when you think someone is going to give you some bad news.

D **1.28 Complete the conversation with phrases from the chart. Listen and check.**

A I just [1] ________ thing! I'm so, so, so [2] ________.
B What did you do?
A I can't [3] ________ I did this, but I just spilled coffee all over your new white rug.
B You what?
A I can't tell you [4] ________!

2 REAL-WORLD STRATEGY

A 1.29 **Listen to two more apologies. What are the people apologizing for?**

RESPOND TO AN APOLOGY

When you respond to an apology and you don't want the person to feel bad, you can use one of these phrases.

It's not the end of the world. *It's really no big deal.* *Don't beat yourself up about it.*

B 1.29 **Read the information in the box above and listen again. Which response does the second person use in each conversation?**

C 1.30 **Complete the conversation with an expression from the box. Listen and check.**

A Hey, where were you last night. We missed you.

B Missed me? Why? Oh no! I forgot about the study group! I can't believe it! It's even on my calendar! And I'm the only one with notes from the workshop! You needed those.

A Don't ______________________ . Just bring them tomorrow.

B I won't forget again. I swear!

3 PRONUNCIATION FOCUS: Saying /s/ at the beginning of a word

A 1.31 **Listen and repeat. Focus on the /s/ sounds.**

1 I can't tell you how **s**orry I am. 2 Don't tell me **s**omebody **s**tole it!

B 1.32 **Listen. Who says the /s/ sound clearly? Write A or B.**

1 sorry ___	3 so ___	5 stole ___
2 somebody ___	4 spilled ___	6 store ___

C PAIR WORK **Say the words in exercise 3B to your partner. Does your partner say the /s/ sound clearly?**

4 SPEAKING

A PAIR WORK **Think of a time when you apologized to someone. What did you do wrong? How did the other person react?**

B PAIR WORK **Act out the situation you described or one of the others below. Student A apologizes. Student B reacts to the apology and tries to make Student A not feel so bad. Then reverse roles: Student B apologizes, and Student A reacts.**

- You drank the last of the milk.
- You forgot to record something on TV.
- You deleted something important from someone's phone or computer.

3.4

BUYER BEWARE!

LESSON OBJECTIVE
- write a product review

1 READING

A ☐

B ☐

C ☐

A **Look at the three pictures. What problems might people have when they buy these things online? Read three stories about online shopping. Match them with the pictures. What were the problems each time? Which story has a happy ending?**

Posts | Related Posts | Search | Log in | Sign up

What is your best or worst online shopping story?

1 I saw a photo of a rug that was perfect for my room. The price was amazing, too – about a quarter of the price of other rugs. So, I bought it. When it came, I was a surprised. The box seemed really small for a rug. When I opened it, I saw why. It wasn't a rug at all – it was a mouse pad! I guess I got what I paid for! (Jensen, Texas)

2 I ordered a beautiful cake for my parents' anniversary – simple and elegant, just what I wanted. The website asked what I wanted written on the cake, and I wrote "nothing," because I wanted to do that myself. When it arrived, I opened the box and, you guessed it, **NOTHING** was written on top, in big black letters! I couldn't believe it! (Bella, Minnesota)

3 It was my grandfather's 75th birthday and I wanted to get him something special. When he was young, he wrote a book about fishing, but he lost his only copy in a fire years before. I tried to find another one at used bookstores and online book sites. One place claimed they could find it. They had no reviews, but I was desperate, so I took a chance. Three days later the book arrived! Grandpa was so happy. It's by far the best birthday present I've ever bought for anyone! (Harry, Chicago)

B READ FOR DETAILS **Read the stories again. Answer the questions.**

1 Why did Jensen want that particular rug?
2 What did Bella want to put on the cake?
3 Why was Harry unsure about the online bookstore?

C PAIR WORK THINK CRITICALLY **Discuss the questions.**

1 Who is to blame for Jensen's and Bella's shopping fails? The store owners? Jensen and Bella themselves? Why?
2 What could Jensen and Bella do differently next time, so they don't repeat their shopping fails?

INSIDER ENGLISH

"You get what you pay for."

People use this phrase when they think they bought something of high quality at a very low price, but in the end they were wrong. The quality is right for that price.

2 WRITING

A **Read the two product reviews. What products are they reviewing? How many stars do you think each reviewer will give their product?**

Product reviews

Reviews | Sign up | Log in | Basket

I was very disappointed with this product.

I bought the case for my summer vacation. I wanted to take photos when I was snorkeling. The case arrived on time and it looked good. I tested it without my phone and it seemed to be working fine.

In fact, it was great for the first 3 times underwater, then suddenly it filled with water while I was filming fish and completely ruined my new phone! It's a complete waste of money! By far my worst purchase ever! DO NOT BUY IT!

☆☆☆☆☆ Rate your purchase

I was really pleased with this product.

They're so comfortable to wear – much more comfortable than my last ones. I like the fact that they include different earpieces so you can find the best fit. And I love the little case – very convenient.

They have great sound quality and are really simple to take phone calls on. They also really block out background noise.

This is such a great set! They are small, portable with their own case, and very good at what they do! Great value for your money! I highly recommend them.

☆☆☆☆☆ Rate your purchase

B WRITING SKILL **Read the reviews again. Find phrases that …**

1 describe the reviewers' feelings.
2 describe the positive features of the product.
3 describe the negative features of the product.
4 give a recommendation.

REGISTER CHECK

Writing a word or sentence in ALL CAPS can be used to express a very strong opinion or feeling. But be careful – it can also suggest an aggressive or angry tone.

C PAIR WORK **Think of a product you have bought recently. Answer the questions and make notes.**

1 Where did you buy it? ______
2 When did you buy it? ______
3 Were you happy with it? Why or why not? ______
4 Would you recommend this product? Why or why not? ______

WRITE IT

D **Write a short review for your product in about 100 words. Read the review to the class. Ask your classmates to guess how many stars you gave your purchase.**

3.5 TIME TO SPEAK
Damage control

LESSON OBJECTIVE
- discuss ways to respond to a negative product review

A **PREPARE** With a partner, look at the picture. What problem are the people having? Did something like this ever happen to you?

B Read the reviews. What problems did each customer have? How do they feel about their purchases? How many stars do you think each customer will give in their product review?

Worst. Vacation. Ever. This was my first vacation on a cruise ship – and my last! I expected a beautiful room with a view of the ocean. It was just the opposite – small, cramped, no window, and it smelled! The food was terrible, too. I can't believe I paid $4,000 for this trip. What a rip-off!

Like Comment ★★★★★

Great bike… if you can put it together. I got this bike for my son's birthday. I knew that I needed to put it together myself, but I didn't know it would be this hard! There's like 100 pieces and ONE page of instructions. It took me five hours to finish it, but now I'm afraid for him to ride it!

Like Comment ★★★★★

C **DECIDE** Form a small group with another pair. Imagine you are the owners of the cruise ship or the do-it-yourself bicycle company. Come up with a plan of action. Discuss the actions in the box and think of others. What will you do? In what order? If the customer still isn't satisfied, what will you do next?

apologize	offer a refund	offer a replacement

D **PRESENT** Form a new group with three new partners. Take turns and present your original group's solution to the new group. Ask and answer questions and offer advice for improvement. Then return to your original group and compare notes. Revise your plan of action.

E **AGREE** Share your group's plan with the class. Discuss which one is best for each company and why. Do you think the customer in each case will be satisfied? Will they change their review? Why or why not?

To check your progress, go to page 153.

USEFUL PHRASES

PREPARE

I had to put together a bookcase once, and it was …

I think the cruise ship passenger feels …

The parent didn't give more than … stars.

DECIDE

First, I think we should apologize to the passenger because …

We could offer a replacement for the bike, but …

PRESENT

We've decided to send them an email and apologize for …

Maybe call them instead of emailing. It's more personal.

REVIEW 1 (UNITS 1–3)

1 VOCABULARY

A **Put the words and phrases into the correct categories. Add three more to each category.**

a salary cut	ambitious	be a fad	be all the rage	boil
break a record	chop	confident	go out of fashion	curious
win a medal	mint	zucchini	gain interest	garlic
time well spent	truthful	enthusiastic	rise to a challenge	ginger
standard of living	rinse	cost of living	set a goal for yourself	stir

1 accomplishments ______
2 describing trends ______
3 food items ______
4 food preparation ______
5 personal qualities ______
6 time and money ______

2 GRAMMAR

A PAIR WORK **Complete the sentences with the correct form of the verbs in parentheses ( ). Then change the sentences so that they are true for you. Compare with a partner.**

1 I ______ (think) of trying the Paleo diet. I ______ (think) it's healthy and natural.
2 After I ______ (finish) this course, I ______ (start) my MBA. I ______ (check) different schools for the past two months.
3 If I ______ (save) enough money, I ______ (go) to Thailand on my next vacation. I ______ (always, want) to visit Bangkok.

B **Complete the paragraph with the words in the box.**

a little | a whole lot | by far | enough | too

I think *Pomodoro* is [1] ______ the best Italian restaurant in town. It's [2] ______ more expensive than the other Italian places around, but the atmosphere is [3] ______ better. On weekends it can get [4] ______ crowded, and you have to wait forever for a table. But the food is worth it. Too bad I don't have [5] ______ money to eat there more often.

C PAIR WORK **What's your favorite restaurant in town? How does it compare to other restaurants?**

3 SPEAKING

A PAIR WORK **Talk to your partner about future goals. Ask and answer the questions.**

What is one of your goals for the near future?
What have you been doing to achieve that goal?
How will your life be different when you accomplish that objective?

B **Summarize what you learned about your partner.**

Ana wants to get a better job. She has been searching job sites, and she has applied for a few jobs. When she gets a better job, she'll move to her own apartment.

4 FUNCTIONAL LANGUAGE

A **Use the words and phrases to complete the conversations at a wedding reception.**

beat yourself up	care for	get you
how sorry	I'm good	know
that'd be great	introduce	
the dumbest	we've met	

1 **A** Hi, I don't think [1] ________________ before. Are you friends with the bride or the groom?

B The bride, Stacy. We work for the same company. And you?

A Stacy is my second cousin. By the way, I'm Lucas. Nice to meet you.

B I'm Tricia. Do you [2] ________________ anyone here?

A Just our relatives.

B Ok, let me [3] ________________ you to a couple of people from the office.

A Thanks!

2 **A** Would you [4] ________________ some more soda?

B No, thanks. [5] ________________ .

A Can I [6] ________________ a piece of the wedding cake?

B Yes, [7] ________________ . Thanks.

3 **A** I'm really sorry, but I just did [8] ________________ thing. I was parking my car and … I hit yours.

B Oh! Well, how bad is the damage?

A Just a scratch. Don't worry; I'll pay for the repairs. I can't tell you [9] ________________ I am!

B That's all right. Don't [10] ________________ about it.

5 SPEAKING

A PAIR WORK **Choose one of the situations below. Act it out in pairs.**

1 Introduce yourself to a new student and offer to introduce him/her to other classmates.

A Hi. I'm [name]. You're new here, right?

B Yes, it's my first day at this school. I'm [name], nice to meet you.

2 You're hosting some classmates at home. Offer them something to drink and eat.

A Can I get you anything to drink?

B Yes, please. Can I have …

3 You dropped your friends' belongings and the screen of her phone broke. Apologize and offer to have it fixed.

A I'm so sorry. You'll never guess what I did.

B What did you do?

B **Change roles and repeat the role play.**

UNIT OBJECTIVES

- speculate about a picture
- talk about viral stories
- exchange and discuss opinions
- write a response to a post about local businesses
- design an ad for a product

GOING GLOCAL

4

START SPEAKING

A **Look at the picture. Where do you think it was taken? How many different signs can you see? What do you think they are selling?**

B **How many different places do you see ads? How many ads do you think you see in one day? How many do you pay attention to? For ideas, watch Seung Geyong's video.**

REAL STUDENT

Is your experience like Seung Geyong's?

4.1 MORE THAN JUST A JERSEY

LESSON OBJECTIVE

- speculate about a picture

1 LANGUAGE IN CONTEXT

A **Look at the infographic. Do you recognize any of the team names? What sport do they represent? What type of information does the infographic give about the teams?**

Real Madrid
Annual revenue: €518 million
Ticket sales: €119 million
Broadcasting rights: €188 million
Sponsorships and merchandising: €211 million

Manchester United
Annual revenue: €424 milllion
Ticket sales: €127 million
Broadcasting rights: €119 million
Sponsorships and merchandising: €178 million

FC Barcelona
Annual revenue: €483 million
Ticket sales: €118 million
Broadcasting rights: €188 million
Sponsorships and merchandising: €177 million

Paris Saint-Germain
Annual revenue: €400 million
Ticket sales: €54 million
Broadcasting rights: €91 million
Sponsorships and merchandising: €255 million

B **Read part of an article on sports marketing. What is a major source of income for these soccer teams? Think of sports teams in your town or country. Do they make money in similar ways?**

Soccer is the world's highest earning sport. You might think that the money comes from ticket sales. But actually, a lot of it comes from sales of merchandise.

Take Real Madrid, for example. Business from its **sponsor** represents one-third of the team's total revenue. For the French team Paris Saint-Germain (PSG), sponsorship and **merchandising** represents over half. That could mean that PSG's **brand** is more valuable than the team itself!

All teams have corporate sponsorship deals, which usually means putting the sponsor's **logo** on the jersey. In the case of Real Madrid and PSG, the same sponsor appears on their jerseys – yes, the Emirates airline company sponsors both!

Sponsorship is everywhere in professional sports. These days if teams don't have sponsors on their jerseys, they can't be taken seriously. Even in the U.S., some NBA teams now have sponsors on their shirts, and TV **commercials** that **advertise** games are also **ads** for the sponsors' **products**.

Because sports team brands are so valuable, authentic jerseys are **status symbols** and **fashion statements**. Other branded products, from coffee mugs to mousepads, also bear the team's (and sponsor's) logo and/or **slogan**. All of this merchandising means fakes are everywhere, too. But if your Real Madrid jersey costs three times the price of one you see on the street, it must be the *Real* thing!

C **Read the article and the infographic again. Check (✓) the statements that are true. Correct the false ones.**

☐ 1 All soccer teams now get most of their revenue from merchandise sales.

☐ 2 It is possible for one company to sponsor two or more teams.

☐ 3 Sponsorship of NBA teams is a new trend.

☐ 4 The sponsor's name only appears on a team's jersey.

! **All the money a company takes in is its *revenue*. The money that is left after all expenses are paid is its *profit*. These are uncountable nouns.**

***Revenue** is up this year, but **profit** is down because of higher costs.*

When a company has many sources of income, they can be countable.

***Revenues** from merchandising and ad sales are down, but **profits** from ticket sales and parking will balance that.*

2 VOCABULARY: Talking about advertising

FIND IT

A 1.33 **Listen and say the words. Find the words from the box in the article and try to figure out what they mean. You can use a dictionary or your phone to help you. Then discuss the questions.**

ad / advertisement	merchandising	advertise	brand
merchandise / products	status symbol	sponsor	logo
fashion statement	commercial	slogan	

What is the difference between …

1 a sponsor (*n*) and sponsor (*v*)?
2 merchandise and merchandising?
3 a brand, a logo, and a slogan?
4 advertise (*v*), an advertisement/ad, and a commercial?
5 a status symbol and a fashion statement?

B **Now go to page 144. Do the vocabulary exercises for 4.1.**

C PAIR WORK **Think of an ad that you really like and one that you really dislike. Why do you feel this way about them? Explain to your partner.**

That commercial is terrible! The slogan is a little song, and it stays in my head for days!

3 GRAMMAR: Modals of speculation

A **Complete the rules. Use the sentences in the grammar box to help you.**

We can use *must, must not, may, might, can't,* and *could* to speculate.

1 When you're not sure that something is true, use ______________, *could*, or *may*.
2 When you're sure that something is true, use ______________.
3 When you're sure that something is not true, use ______________ and *must not*.

Modals of speculation

You **might** think that the money comes from ticket sales.
If it's three times the price, then it **must** be real.
If teams don't have sponsors, they **can't** be taken seriously.

ACCURACY CHECK

Don't use *can* for speculation.

They ~~can~~ be the best soccer team this season. ✗
They might be the best soccer team this season. ✓

B **Complete the sentences with an appropriate modal of speculation. Then check your accuracy.**

1 They ______________ be a very good soccer team. They haven't won a single game this season!
2 They ______________ be the best soccer team this year, but I'm not sure.
3 They ______________ be the best soccer team this year. They've won everything!

C **Now go to page 132. Look at the grammar chart and do the grammar exercise for 4.1.**

4 SPEAKING

A GROUP WORK **Look at the picture. Speculate about what is happening. Who makes the most interesting guess?**

It can't be an actual game. It must be during practice.

He might be teaching the dog to play soccer.

4.2 VIRAL STORIES

LESSON OBJECTIVE
- talk about viral stories

1 LANGUAGE IN CONTEXT

A 1.34 **Look at the picture. Do you know about this image? What do you think the story is about? Listen to the podcast and check your answers.**

1.34 Audio script

Today we're talking about viral stories and their impact. The internet is full of viral stories – stories that we see and share, and then others reshare, and reshare, etc. Surprisingly, viral stories are often not about **celebrities.** You don't have to be a famous **entertainer** or a cultural **icon** to go viral.

Take the story of Murtaza Ahmadi. Murtaza was an Afghani boy who made a copy of his **hero** Lionel Messi's jersey out of a plastic bag. Someone took a photo. It went viral and changed Murtaza's life. He got to travel to Qatar where his dreams came true and he met Messi.

Stories which warm our hearts are not the only ones that can go viral. Many are just silly or amusing. There are countless online **performers** that we only know thanks to YouTube. Many are people who don't even have any special talent.

There are people like Matt McAllister, who became famous for wearing 155 t-shirts at the same time! His video has had over 17.5 million views. It's not going to change the world, but it's something that might make us laugh. And sometimes, maybe that's enough.

B 1.34 **What categories do viral stories or videos usually fit in? Listen again and check.**

C PAIR WORK **What people can you think of who have become famous overnight and/or online? Do you think they deserve to be famous? Why or why not?**

2 VOCABULARY: Talking about people in the media

A

B

C

FIND IT

A 1.35 **Listen and say the words. Which words describe the people in the pictures? Look up any terms you don't know. You can use a dictionary or your phone to help you.**

1 audience C	5 DJ ___	9 icon ___
2 celebrity ___	6 entertainer ___	10 model ___
3 comedian ___	7 filmmaker ___	11 movie producer ___
4 designer ___	8 hero ___	12 performer ___

B PAIR WORK **Think of one person for each word.**

A celebrity can be anybody who is famous for something. For example, Stephen Hawking was a scientist, but he was definitely a celebrity.

C **Now go to page 144. Do the vocabulary exercise for 4.2.**

D **Complete the sentences so that they are true for you.**

1 A performer I really admire is …
2 My hero from childhood was …
3 An icon in my culture / country is …
4 A DJ I love to listen to is …
5 My favorite filmmaker is …
6 A well-known fashion designer here is …

3 GRAMMAR: Subject and object relative clauses

A **Look at the excerpt from the audio script. Then complete the rules.**

> The internet is full of viral stories – stories **that we see and share, and then others reshare, and reshare, etc.**
>
> Take the story of Murtaza Ahmadi. Murtaza was an Afghani boy **who made a copy of his hero Lionel Messi's jersey out of a plastic bag.** Someone took a photo. It went viral and changed Murtaza's life. He got to travel to Qatar **where his dreams came true.**

1 Relative clauses give extra information about ________________, things, or places.
2 A relative clause begins with a relative pronoun: *who, which,* ________________, or *where.*
3 In subject relative clauses, the relative pronoun is the subject of the clause and is always followed by a **noun or pronoun** / **verb**.
4 In object relative clauses, the relative pronoun is the object of the clause and is followed by a **noun or pronoun** / **verb**.

B **Now go to page 133. Look at the grammar chart and do the grammar exercise for 4.2.**

C PAIR WORK **Choose three items from exercise 2D. Ask your partner to tell you about them.**

Tell me about a performer who you really admire.

I really admire Carlos Vives. He's so talented. He can sing and he can act!

4 SPEAKING

Are your opinions similar to Alessandra's?

A PAIR WORK **Look at these sentences. Do you agree or disagree with them? Think of examples to support your opinion. For ideas, watch Alessandra's video.**

1 Most people who become famous on the internet have no real talent.
2 It's too easy to be a celebrity these days. In the past, you had to be really good!
3 It's great that we can all become stars. Anyone can be discovered – it's more democratic!
4 The media spend too much time talking about celebrity gossip. It's boring and unimportant.
5 I love all the news about celebrities. It's funny and distracts me from all the serious news in the world.

4.3 THAT'S A GOOD POINT, BUT ...

LESSON OBJECTIVE
- exchange and discuss opinions

1 FUNCTIONAL LANGUAGE

A 1.36 **Look at the picture. What are the two people doing? How does each person feel? Why do you think they feel that way? Read and listen to their conversation. Were you correct?**

1.36 Audio script

A Colombia is playing Uruguay this afternoon, want to watch it?

B Soccer? Well, not really. **As I see it**, soccer is just a bunch of guys running around for 90 minutes to score two, maybe three goals. To be honest, **I find it** really boring.

A **Now, just a second.** That's not fair at all. Even if the score is low, there's *a lot* happening. Sports are about strategy.

B OK, **that's a good point, but** 90 minutes? The strategy is that interesting?

A Yes, absolutely. And soccer is a cultural experience, too. **I really think** you'd enjoy that side of it at least.

B **It's not so much that** I'm not interested, **it's just that** I don't really understand the game. I just feel lost when I watch it.

A OK, **but the thing is,** you have to watch a sport to understand it. You like basketball now, but you didn't before we went to some games.

B **That's true, but** basketball was more familiar to me. With soccer, you're going to have to explain everything!

A I have to talk about soccer all afternoon? Hey, no problem.

B **Complete the chart with the bold expressions from the conversation.**

Exchanging opinions	Discussing opinions
As I [1] ______ it, ...	Now, just a [5] ______ ...
I [2] ______ it /that (really boring).	That's a good [6] ______, but ...
I [3] ______ think (you'd enjoy it).	But the [7] ______ is, ...
It's not so [4] ______ that ..., it's just that ...	That's [8] ______, but ...

C 1.37 **Complete the conversations with expressions from the chart. Then listen and check.**

1 A Soccer is a multimillion dollar sport now, and money is destroying the game.
  B Now, [1] ______ – destroying the game? That's a bit strong.
  A Maybe, but I really [2] ______ it's true. It's all about money now.

2 A Advertising is such a creative industry these days, don't you think?
  B I guess, but I [3] ______ it kind of sad that so many talented people only ever do that.
  A Well, it's not [4] ______ their talent is wasted, it's just that they use it in a practical way.

D PAIR WORK **Practice the conversations above with a partner. Then have a new conversation about something you feel strongly about using the same expressions.**

I like smartwatches, but the thing is, I just don't like to wear jewelry.

2 REAL-WORLD STRATEGY

A 1.38 **Listen to two people talking about movies. What do they disagree about?**

MAKE OPINIONS MORE EMPHATIC

When we disagree strongly with someone, we often want to express an opinion more emphatically.

That's not true *at all*.

I couldn't disagree more.

You have it *all* wrong.

B 1.38 **Read the box above. Complete the conversation with expressions from the box. Listen and check.**

A Hey, do you want to go see that new superhero movie with me?

B A comic book movie? Uh, I'll pass. They're all so dumb.

A What? I [1] ______________________. The special effects are great, and they're really funny.

B Funny? Come on. They're written for 12-year-olds.

A That's [2] ______________________. Take *Deadpool*, for instance. That movie's very funny, and the jokes are definitely written for adults.

B If you say so. Personally, I'd much rather see a spy movie, like James Bond. They're exciting, but realistic.

A You've got to be kidding. Evil villains and spy gadgets? Now, that's silly.

B No, no. You [3] ______________________. That's the old ones. The new ones are really good.

C PAIR WORK **Student A: Give an opinion about a sports team, a movie, or an entertainer that you know. Student B: Disagree emphatically with A. Then switch roles and have a similar conversation.**

3 PRONUNCIATION FOCUS: Saying the vowel sounds /ɔ/ and /ɑ/

A 1.39 **Listen and repeat the two different vowel sounds.**

/ɔ/ **a**ll That's not fair at **all**. /ɑ/ s**o**ccer S**o**ccer is a cultural experience.

B 1.40 **Listen. Write A for words with /ɔ/. Write B for words with /ɑ/.**

1 **au**dience ____ 3 m**o**del ____ 5 sp**o**nsor ____

2 n**o**t ____ 4 **aw**esome ____ 6 c**au**ght ____

C 1.41 PAIR WORK **Listen to the conversations. Then practice with a partner.**

1 **A** Want to watch s**o**ccer this afternoon?

B Sure. There's an **aw**esome game between England and Argentina.

2 **A** Why don't you like going to c**o**ncerts?

B Being in a big **au**dience makes me nervous.

4 SPEAKING

A PAIR WORK **Choose <u>two</u> of the subjects to talk about. Practice giving opinions about the topic and responding to them, sometimes emphatically.**

an ad on TV right now a global brand a sports team (your choice) a viral video

What do you think of that funny car ad with the big chicken? Kids really like it.

That's true, but kids don't buy cars. I really don't think it's a good ad.

4.4 BUILDING A BRAND

LESSON OBJECTIVE

- write a response to a post about local businesses

1 LISTENING

A PAIR WORK **Look at the sandals. Do you recognize this brand? Where is it from? Is it a local brand or a global brand?**

B 1.42 LISTEN FOR GIST **Listen to a report about the creation of the global brand, *Havaianas*. Check (✓) the ideas that are mentioned.**

- ☐ **1** origins of the brand
- ☐ **2** the advertising plan
- ☐ **3** international growth
- ☐ **4** problems in the business
- ☐ **5** how Havaianas are made

C 1.42 LISTEN FOR DETAILS **Listen to the report again. Choose the correct words to make true statements.**

1. *Everybody / Only some people* in Brazil wore Havaianas in the 1960s.
2. The company *only sells flip-flops / sells other items.*
3. Havaianas became a luxury item *in / outside of* Brazil.
4. The price of a pair of Havaianas in Brazil is *much less / much more* than in international markets.
5. The international success of this product is due to *the product itself / its marketing.*

INSIDER ENGLISH

Flip-flops get their name from the sound they make as you walk in them: *flip-flop, flip-flop*. There are a number of words in English that come from the sound something makes: *clap* your hands; a dog's *bark*.

FIND IT

D THINK CRITICALLY PAIR WORK **Havaianas were originally workers' shoes and are now a global fashion item. What other companies can you think of that started local and went global? Share the story with the class. You can use your phone to help you.**

> Levi's jeans were for cowboys and farmers. In the 1960s, young people started wearing them too. Now people wear them almost anywhere.

2 PRONUNCIATION: Listening for topic organization

A 1.43 **Listen to extracts from the report. Write the words that receive the most stress.**

1 ______ / ______ ______

2 ______

3 ______

B **Choose the correct phrase to complete the sentence.**

Stress is often used to indicate the speaker is talking about *the same topic / a new topic.*

3 WRITING

A **Read the post on social media about the impact of global brands on local communities. What change does the writer describe? From whose point of view is this written?**

Posts | Related Posts | Search | Log in | Sign up

Recently, an international company opened a couple of convenience stores right on Main Street. There weren't any chain stores like this before, only small, family-run stores that sell local products. As a result, our town had a nice traditional feel.

These new stores are ugly, but they stay open late. Due to the large number of people who work the late shift at local factories, these stores are sometimes their only option for grocery shopping. Also, thanks to the fact that they're part of a large chain, they can offer a bigger range of products at lower prices than independent stores.

Consequently, a lot of the independent stores downtown are closing. They just can't compete. I think this is a real shame, as we are losing more than stores, we're losing an important part of the community.

Is the same thing happening where you are? Share examples from your community.

B **Read the post again. What reasons does the writer give for the new stores' success? Does he have a positive or negative opinion of the changes in his town?**

C WRITING SKILL **There are five expressions in the post that mark reasons and consequences. Find them and write them below based on similar meaning.**

1 because (of): ______
______
______

2 so: ______
______

D PAIR WORK **Think of an example from your community. Consider the following questions:**

- Which new stores have appeared and which have disappeared?
- What are some reasons for the success of the new stores?
- How do the new stores affect local employment and/or local traditions?
- Is it, generally speaking, a change for the better or for the worse?

WRITE IT

E **Write a response to the post using your community as an example. Write 100–120 words. Include a description of the new business(es), the old business(es), and the reasons for and consequences of the change.**

F **Read your response to the class. Do your classmates agree with you? Why or why not?**

A big supermarket has opened in the downtown area. It sells food at cheaper prices and they have more choice. As a result, the little shops selling fruit and vegetables have closed. It's not good for the community at all.

4.5 TIME TO SPEAK
Design an ad

LESSON OBJECTIVE
- design an ad for a product

A **RESEARCH** **Read about advertising techniques. With a partner, think of types of products (toothpaste, running shoes, medicine, etc.) and discuss which techniques are typically used in their ads.**

Ads for high-end watches often have athletes in them. So that's an endorsement by a celebrity.

1 Endorsement: a respected expert or celebrity supports the product (for example, a movie star does commercials for a brand of shampoo, a famous soccer player puts his name on a new cologne for men)

2 Association of ideas: the product is connected to a particular idea (for example, cars = freedom)

3 "The camera never lies": the product looks visually attractive or appealing (for example, the perfect burger)

4 Technology: the product is (or uses) the latest and best technology (for example, the latest generation smartphone)

5 Guilt: the ad makes the customer feel bad for not having the product already (for example, a safer car seat for children)

B **DECIDE** **Work in small groups to design an ad for a product. Choose one of the products from the box or think of another one. Decide on the central idea or main image for your ad and also the technique(s) that would be best to sell your product. You can draw it or write a plan for it.**

car cosmetics food product jewelry sports equipment TV show

Our product is jeans. We should use a DJ in a club where people are dancing. The technique might be association of ideas.

C **PRESENT** **Explain your group's idea to a student from another group. Ask for their feedback and take notes. Rejoin your group and share all the feedback. Work with your group to refine and improve your ad. Be sure your final ad includes the following:**

- a main image (or an idea for one)
- a slogan
- a short text to accompany the ad

D **AGREE** **Present your ads to the class and explain the technique(s) you chose to use. Watch the other presentations and decide which one is the most effective and most original. Explain your opinion.**

To check your progress, go to page 154.

USEFUL PHRASES

RESEARCH
The ad for … uses …
The people in the ad look like they …
Ads for … make me feel …

DECIDE
How about a food product?
Let's use the … technique.
We could use images of …

PRESENT
The central idea of our product is …
The advertising technique we plan to use is …

UNIT OBJECTIVES

- discuss different types of stories
- talk about plans and changes to plans in the past
- react to problems and disappointing news
- write a formal apology
- tell a story about a chance meeting

TRUE STORIES

5

START SPEAKING

A Look at the picture. What kind of story do you think she is telling? How do you know?

B When was the last time you heard a good story? What was it about? Who told it to you?

C Who is the best storyteller you know? What kind of stories do they tell? For ideas, watch Maryne's video.

REAL STUDENT

Is Maryne's favorite storyteller similar to yours?

5.1 THAT'S ANOTHER STORY!

LESSON OBJECTIVES:
- discuss different types of stories

1 VOCABULARY: Describing stories

A 1.44 **Look at the different kinds of stories in the box. Listen and say the words. Which usually involve a happy ending? strong emotions? sad events?**

coming-of-age story	family saga	feel-good story	hard-luck story
horror story	human interest story	love story	mystery
personal tragedy	success story	tall tale	tearjerker

B **Now go to page 145. Do the vocabulary exercises for 5.1.**

C PAIR WORK **Think of three stories you've heard about recently on TV, in the news, or from a friend. Tell the main events and decide which story type(s) best describes each one.**

2 LANGUAGE IN CONTEXT

A **Read the introduction. What's the name of the company? What is a "pitch"? What services does the company offer? Read the whole page to check your answers.**

Sell your story!

Writers, are you tired of rejection letters? Maybe it isn't you. Maybe it's your pitch. Let PitchMasters create a short, catchy pitch for your story that no publisher could resist. Just tell us the plot, and get ready to be famous!

Comments

Crazy4wordz
My story is about a man and a woman who had secretly loved each other for years, but they'd never even spoken. Finally, the woman writes him a love letter. The next day he's in a terrible accident …

Sarahthewriter
I have the best idea for a story. It's about a woman who had written stories for years but hadn't had the courage to submit them. One day, her dad is cleaning out her old room and finds a story that she had written as a teenager. He sends it in, and it gets published! It sells millions! Basically, it's my story (I hope).

Starvingartist
My story will really scare you. It's a whodunit about a man who moves into a new house. But he doesn't know that the husband and wife who lived there before had died in the house. Pretty soon he starts hearing strange noises at night and …

B PAIR WORK **Read the plot summaries again. Which story types from exercise 1A best describe them?**

C PAIR WORK **Discuss the questions.**
- Which of the three story ideas do you think has the most interesting plot? Why?
- What kinds of stories do you generally enjoy? Why?
- Are there any kinds of stories you generally don't like? Why?

INSIDER ENGLISH

A *whodunit* is a type of mystery. *Whodunit* is a playful way to say "Who has done it?" (*who is guilty of the crime?*)

3 GRAMMAR: Past perfect

A **Choose the correct words to complete the rules. Use the sentences in the grammar box to help you.**

1 The past perfect is used to talk about things that happened **before** / **after** another event in the past.

2 When there are two completed events in the past, use the **simple past** / **past perfect** for the event that happened after the first event.

3 To form the past perfect, use ***had*** / ***would*** + past participle.

Past perfect

It's about a man and a woman who **had** secretly **loved** each other for years, but they**'d** never even **spoken**.

A woman **had written** stories for years but **hadn't had** the courage to submit them.

B **There are two actions in each sentence. Circle the action that happened first.**

1 We had been there an hour before he finally met with us.

2 When the game finally ended, our team had given up seven goals.

3 They had left by the time we arrived.

4 He was surprised that he had never seen that photo before.

C **Now go to page 133. Look at the grammar chart and do the grammar exercise for 5.1.**

D PAIR WORK **Complete the sentences so they are true for you. Use the past perfect. Read your sentences to a partner. Ask questions to find out more about your partner's stories.**

1 When I got home last night, ________________ had already ________________.

2 It was the first time I had ever ________________. I loved it!

3 I had never ________________ before, and I'm never going to do it again!

4 SPEAKING

FIND IT

A **Think of a person whose life would make an interesting book or movie. It can be someone you know or a celebrity or historical figure. Add background information using the past perfect. You can use your phone to look up details about the person.**

B GROUP WORK **Tell your stories to the group. Which of the stories did you find most interesting? Why?**

I think a story about Manuela Saenz would make a great movie. She had been married to an Englishman, but she left her husband in 1822 to fight with Simon Bolivar. She'd already been involved in the fight for independence for several years and …

5.2 LAST-MINUTE-ITIS

LESSON OBJECTIVE
- talk about plans and changes to plans in the past

1 LANGUAGE IN CONTEXT

A 1.45 **Look at the text message. Do you often send or receive text messages like this? Listen to two friends discussing another friend, Suzie. What excuses does Suzie make? Do her friends believe her?**

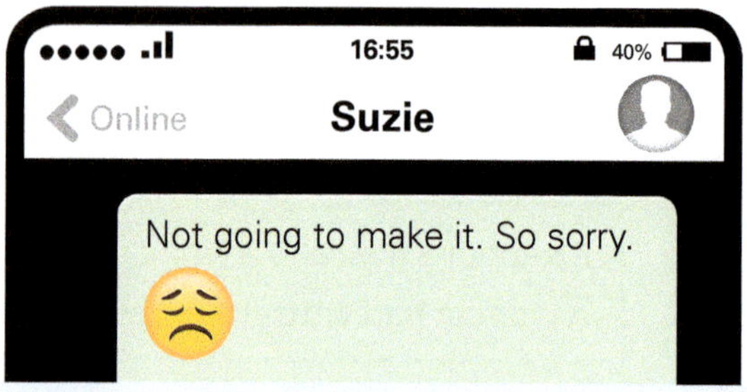

1.45 Audio script

A What's up with Suzie lately? We were going to get together last night. I was really looking forward to it, but at the last minute, she texted that she was held up at work and to go ahead without her. I ended up just staying home.

B Last week, she really messed things up for me, too! I'd bought tickets to a concert. About an hour before we were supposed to meet, she texted, said she was sorry to let me down, but she couldn't go. She said her sister had split up with her boyfriend, and she had to hang out with her and try to cheer her up.

A No way! She's just making up excuses.

B I know! And it's always in a text.

A I'm about ready to give up on her!

INSIDER ENGLISH

We use the expressions *What's up with … ?* and *Something's up* to talk about problems.

2 VOCABULARY: Making and breaking plans

A 1.46 **Find the verb phrases in the conversation and complete them below. Then listen and check.**

1 be held ________
2 cheer ________
3 end ________
4 ________ together
5 give up ________
6 go ________
7 hang out ________
8 let someone ________
9 look ________ to
10 make ________
11 mess ________
12 split ________

B **Now go to page 145. Do the vocabulary exercises for 5.2.**

C GROUP WORK **Do the quiz. Which of you suffers most from last-minute-itis? How do you feel when people cancel or change plans at the last minute? Do you think it's rude? Why or why not?**

Do you suffer from *last-minute-itis?*

How many times did you do each of these things in the last week? Be honest!

- text a friend at the last minute to change plans
- cancel plans with friends because you didn't feel like going
- text that you were running late
- forget to show up for a meeting because you didn't put it in your phone.

3 GRAMMAR: *was/were going to; was/were supposed to*

A **Choose the correct words to complete the rules. Use the sentences in the grammar box to help you.**

1 The forms *was/were going to* and *was/were supposed to* describe an action that **was completed** / **was planned** in the past.

2 They are often used to say that a plan **happened** / **didn't happen**.

3 They are often followed by ***and*** / ***but*** and an explanation.

> ***was/were going to; was/were supposed to***
>
> We **were going to** get together last night, but she was held up at work.
>
> An hour before we **were supposed to** meet, she texted me to cancel.

B **Now go to page 134. Look at the grammar chart and do the grammar exercise for 5.2.**

C PAIR WORK **Read the two situations. What was the original plan? How do you know? Summarize using *was/were supposed to* or *was/were going to*. Check your accuracy.**

1 We were all packed and ready to leave, when it started to rain really heavily. There was no point in going. We didn't want to put up a tent in the rain!

2 We apologized to the people who had come to the meeting and took them for coffee. Then we set up a conference call and had the meeting over Skype.

> ✓ **ACCURACY** CHECK
>
> **Remember not to drop the verb *be* in phrases with *going to* and *supposed to*.**
>
> *The show ~~supposed~~ to start at 7:30.* ✗
>
> *The show was supposed to start at 7:30.* ✓

4 SPEAKING

A **Think about a time when your plans had to change for some reason. Use the questions below to help you. For ideas, watch Seung Geyong's video.**

- What were you going to do?
- What went wrong?
- What did you end up doing?

REAL STUDENT

Did something similar happen to you?

B PAIR WORK **Tell your partner what happened and listen to your partner's story. Ask follow-up questions to get more information.**

> I was going to visit my cousin in Miami. I had bought the tickets and everything. But when I got to the airport, I realized that I had forgotten my passport at home ...

5.3 THERE MUST BE A MISTAKE!

LESSON OBJECTIVE
- react to problems and disappointing news

1 FUNCTIONAL LANGUAGE

A 1.47 PAIR WORK **How would you describe the restaurant in the picture? Why would you choose to go to a place like this? Read and listen to the conversation between a customer and a restaurant host. What was supposed to happen? What's the problem?**

1.47 Audio script

A Hi there. Anderson, party of six, for 8 o'clock.
B I'm sorry, sir, but we don't have a reservation in that name.
A **I don't understand**, I made the reservation myself. **Can you check again, please?**
B Hmm, no, it isn't here.
A **There must be some kind of mistake.** I called last week. Is there a table for six we can have?
B I'm afraid there isn't, sir. We're fully booked.
A But **there must be something you can do.** We're supposed to celebrate my wife's birthday tonight. **I'd like to speak to the manager, please.**
B I'm afraid the manager isn't here at the moment, but let me check … Ah! We have a table at 9. Would that be OK?
A Well, I guess it will have to be OK.
B I'm very sorry for the mistake. We'll give your table some appetizers as an apology.
A That would be nice. Thank you. **I'm glad it's settled.**

B **Complete the chart with the bold expressions from the conversation.**

! For reservations, a group of people is often called a *party*.

Reacting to a problem	Asking for a solution	Accepting a solution
I don't [1] __________. Would you mind taking another look? Can you [2] __________ again, please? There must be some kind of [3] __________.	There must be [4] __________ you can do. I'd like to speak to the [5] __________, please. Is there someone else I could speak to about this, please?	That'll work. I'm glad it's / that's [6] __________.

C 1.48 **Complete the conversation with expressions from the chart. Listen and check. Then practice it with a partner.**

A I'm sorry, sir, but I'm afraid you aren't going to be able to take this flight.
B What? I [1] __________.
A The flight was over-booked. There aren't any seats available.
B There [2] __________ something you can do.
A Well, we can put you on the next flight. It leaves in two hours.
B Just two hours? Oh, OK, [3] __________. I'll just be a little late for the meeting.

2 REAL-WORLD STRATEGY

A 1.49 **Listen to two conversations. What's the problem in each?**

ACCEPTING BAD NEWS

Sometimes there is nothing you can do about a bad situation or result, and you just have to accept it. Use these phrases to show you're disappointed, but you accept the situation.

That's not what I was hoping to hear, but what can you do?

Well, it is what it is.

Well, that's life.

That's too bad, but hey, …

B 1.50 **Read the information about accepting bad news. Use an appropriate expression to complete the conversations. Listen and check your answers.**

1 **A** I'm really sorry, ma'am, but there are no more tickets for tonight's show.
B Are you sure? What about tomorrow?
A I'm afraid there are no tickets left for tomorrow either.
B Oh, no. ________________ . Thanks anyway.

2 **A** Can I pick up my laptop later today?
B No, I'm sorry sir. It won't be ready until tomorrow.
A ________________ , but hey, I still have my phone!

C PAIR WORK **Practice the conversations with a partner.**

REGISTER CHECK

When something goes wrong at a business – even if the worker has made a big mistake, you should use a calm, polite tone and keep your language rather formal. Shouting or showing anger will make people less interested in helping you.

I'm sorry, sir, but I just rented out the last car.

I don't understand. I reserved a car for today online. May I speak with the manager, please?

3 PRONUNCIATION FOCUS: Saying consonants at the end of a word

A 1.51 **Listen and repeat. Focus on the consonant sounds at the end of the words.**

1 Can you check again, please?
2 There must be some kind of mistake.

B 1.52 **Listen. Who pronounces the consonant sound at the end of the word clearly? Write A or B.**

1 check ____
2 mistake ____
3 celebrate ____
4 ticket ____
5 bad ____
6 glad ____

C PAIR WORK **Say the words in exercise 3B to your partner. Does your partner say the consonant sounds clearly?**

4 SPEAKING

A PAIR WORK **Look at the list of disappointing situations. Choose one and act it out. One person gives bad news and the other reacts. Switch roles and act out another one, or think of a new situation.**

- You just missed your train. You ask the guard on the platform about the next train. There isn't one until tomorrow!
- You're buying a T-shirt for your sister for her birthday. They don't have her size in the shop. You can order one, but it won't arrive in time.
- You took your phone to be repaired. You go to pick it up. They tell you they can't fix it.

5.4 THE PERFECT APOLOGY?

LESSON OBJECTIVE
- write a formal apology

1 READING

A PAIR WORK **Look at the picture. What problems do you think this might cause for air travel? Read the article about an airline that made a big mistake. What was the mistake?**

THE PERFECT APOLOGY

In the winter of 2007, the U.S. was hit by a heavy snowstorm, which caused hundreds of flights to be canceled. At one airport, passengers who had already taken their seats on Jet Blue planes before their flight was canceled had to stay there, inside the plane but on the ground, for 11 hours. People were furious with Jet Blue. But Jet Blue's mistake is not what makes this story memorable.

The CEO quickly made a public corporate apology:

> Words cannot express how truly sorry we are for the anxiety, frustration, and inconvenience that you, your family, friends, and colleagues experienced … We know we failed last week … You deserved better—a lot better … and we let you down.

His apology was heartfelt. He admitted that Jet Blue had handled the situation poorly and recognized that a lot of people had suffered. He also offered every passenger compensation to make up for it, which cost his company more than $20 million. And he didn't stop there. He openly explained what had gone wrong and how the company was going to make sure it never happened again.

In short, he followed the three rules for a perfect apology: 1) say you're sorry; 2) promise it will never happen again; 3) do something to make up for it. These are rules that anyone can, and should, follow.

B INTERPRETING ATTITUDE **Read the article again. Why does the writer think the apology was so good? Underline the positive adjectives and adverbs he uses to show his opinion.**

C UNDERSTANDING MEANING FROM CONTEXT **Find words in the text with the following meanings:**

1 (*v*) experience pain or an unpleasant emotion ________
2 (*adj*) associated with business ________
3 (*n*) money you get when you have had a problem ________
4 (*phr v*) reduce the bad effect of something ________

D THINK CRITICALLY **Why did the CEO make a public apology? Is it usual for corporations to apologize when they make a mistake? Can you think of any recent examples? Is a public apology enough? Why or why not?**

2 WRITING

A Read an excerpt from another famous corporate apology. In what way is it similar to the apology in the Jet Blue article? Does it follow the three rules for a good apology?

To our customers,

At Apple, we strive to make world-class products that deliver the best experience possible to our customers. With the launch of our new Maps last week, we fell short on this commitment. We are extremely sorry for the frustration this has caused our customers and we are doing everything we can to make Maps better.

GLOSSARY

strive (*v*) try hard
deliver (*v*) give
launch (*n*) first release
fall short (*phrase*) not do as well as you should

B Read the apology again. What does "this commitment" refer to in the second sentence? Which of the phrases below could you use to replace "this commitment"?

our agreement	our mistake
this goal	this promise to you

C WRITING SKILL **Look at this short corporate apology. Use one of the phrases in the box above to avoid repetition in the second sentence.**

Last week our company accidentally released the personal data of some of our customers. We are deeply sorry for releasing the personal data for some of our customers.

FIND IT

D **Look at the situation below, or go online and find a similar situation that has been in the news recently. Answer the questions.**

A car company has discovered a dangerous mechanical problem and must tell their customers. They are offering to replace those cars with new ones.

- What's the problem?
- Who does it affect? In what way?

WRITE IT

E PAIR WORK **Write a public apology from the CEO of the car company. Write about 80 words. Remember to avoid repetition where possible.**

5.5 TIME TO SPEAK
A chance meeting

LESSON OBJECTIVE
- tell a story about a chance meeting

A **PREPARE** Look at the picture. What's happening? Where do you think they're going to meet? What are they going to do?

B Work in groups. Group A: Go to page 157. Group B: Go to page 159. Follow the instructions.

C **DISCUSS** Work with a partner from the other group. Tell each other your back stories. What do you think the two people said to each other on the phone? What do you think happens next? How does the story end?

D **PRESENT** Join another pair of students. Act out the story from the time they meet through your proposed ending. Ask and answer questions. How different are your two endings?

E Share your stories with the class. How many different endings are there? Look at the real end of the story on page 158. Did anyone get it right?

To check your progress, go to page 154.

USEFUL PHRASES

PREPARE
They are going to …
I think they're planning to …

DISCUSS
I think they're probably going to …
And then they might …
They definitely won't …

PRESENT
So this is what I know: …
She/He was supposed to …
But instead she/he …
From the woman's/man's point of view, …

UNIT OBJECTIVES

- discuss charities and volunteer work
- discuss acts of kindness in your community
- offer, refuse, and accept help with something
- write a report about a community project
- design an urban project for your community

COMMUNITY ACTION

6

START SPEAKING

A **Look at the picture of a volunteer organization. What do you think they're building? Who do you think they're building it for? Use your phone to learn more about this organization.**

B **Would you participate in a program like the one in the picture? Why or why not?**

C **Building homes for others is an "act of kindness." What other good deeds or acts of kindness can you do in your community? For ideas, watch Maryne's video.**

REAL STUDENT

Are your answers the same as Maryne's?

6.1 HELPING OUT

LESSON OBJECTIVE

- discuss charities and volunteer work

1 LANGUAGE IN CONTEXT

A 1.53 **Look at the logo. What do you think the organization does? Listen to the three people describe the organizations they are involved with. Which one matches the logo?**

SOCIAL BITE

1.53 Audio script

Hiro ______ "I **got involved with** this organization because I wanted to help people in my neighborhood. The Center is designed to **bring elderly people together** and keep them active and interested in life. I **volunteer** at the Center and I also visit people in their homes. You **get to know** them, and they really **connect with** you and trust you."

Sandra ______ "I **help out** at a shelter for stray animals that opened a few years ago. I **joined** last year, and I help **take care of** abandoned pets. Some people **donate** money to help us, but supplies are always needed, too. I love the work here because I'm making a difference."

Kemal ______ "Second chances aren't given out all the time, so I know I'm lucky. I was unemployed and homeless, but then I found the café. This place was set up to help people like me learn a practical skill. I serve food, but now I also **take part in** training sessions for new employees. This place changed my life, so I want to **pass on** things I've learned and help others."

GLOSSARY

shelter (*n*) a place that protects people or animals
stray (*adj*) living on the streets with no owner (for dogs and cats)

2 VOCABULARY: Discussing good works

A PAIR WORK 1.54 **Look at the bold words in the audio script. Match them with the correct definitions below. Listen and check.**

1 assist with something: *help out*
2 find that you have something in common with somebody: ______
3 learn more about someone: ______
4 look after someone or something: ______
5 share information with someone: ______
6 give money or other things to help an organization: ______
7 do something without receiving money: ______
8 participate in an activity: ______
9 become a member or work with an organization: ______ or ______
10 help people socialize: ______

B Now go to page 146. Do the vocabulary exercises for 6.1.

C PAIR WORK **Answer the questions.**

- What volunteer organization is special to you? When did you get involved with it?
- What group would you like to join someday? Why?

I'd like to get involved with Friends of the Earth, because I'm very worried about climate change.

3 GRAMMAR: Present and past passive

A **Look at the sentences in the grammar box. Underline the main action in each sentence. Do you know who or what did this action? Is it important to know?**

Present and past passive

The Center is designed to bring elderly people together.

Supplies are always needed at the shelter.	The café was set up to help people learn a skill.
Second chances aren't given out all the time.	My life was changed by this place.

B **Now go to page 134. Look at the grammar chart and do the grammar exercise for 6.1.**

C PAIR WORK **Complete the sentences with the correct passive form of the verbs in the box. Then check your accuracy. Some sentences have more than one correct answer.**

base	coordinate	donate	focus
found	organize	produce	support

✓ ACCURACY CHECK

In passive sentences, the verb *to be* always agrees with the subject.

Our program ~~are~~ designed for elderly people. ✗

Our program is designed for elderly people. ✓

Friends of the Earth (FOE) is an international network of environmental organizations. It [1] ______________ in 1969 by Robert O. Anderson. Originally, it [2] ______________ in North America and Europe, but now it [3] ______________ on the developing world. One of their biggest campaigns against climate change was "The Big Ask." The project [4] ______________ by many celebrities, including musicians such as Paul McCartney. A song called "A Love Song to the Earth" [5] ______________, and all the profits [6] ______________ to FOE. Today, some activities [7] ______________ at the international level but a lot of different protests [8] ______________ by local FOE groups all over the world.

4 SPEAKING

A PAIR WORK **Look at the two logos. Do you know what organizations they stand for? What do you know about them?**

MEDECINS SANS FRONTIERES
DOCTORS WITHOUT BORDERS

WWF

FIND IT

B **Student A: Go to page 158. Student B: Go to page 157.** **Read about your organization and underline key information. You can also look up more information on your phone.**

C PAIR WORK **Complete the questions about your organization with the verbs in parentheses ( ). Then ask and answer the questions with your partner.**

1 When ______________ the organization ______________ ? (found)

2 Where ______________ it ______________ ? (base)

3 How ______________ it ______________ ? (fund)

4 What ______________ its work ______________ ? (focus on)

6.2 RANDOM ACTS OF KINDNESS

LESSON OBJECTIVE

- discuss acts of kindness in your community

1 LANGUAGE IN CONTEXT

A **When you borrow money and then return it, you "pay it back." But what do you think it means to "pay it forward"? Circle your answer. Then read the review to check your answer.**

a Be generous to everyone you meet and money will come to you someday.

b If someone is nice to you, then you should be nice to someone else next.

c When you don't owe anyone anything, you feel good about yourself.

BOOK REVIEWS Home News Reviews Account

Paying It Forward offers a stunning lesson on kindness

1 ______________________

In the book, *Paying It Forward: How one cup of coffee could change the world*, a university professor describes an experiment with **acts of kindness**. She tried to **lend a helping hand** to a stranger – offering her umbrella or giving someone coins for a parking meter. In return, she asked those people to do a nice thing for someone else.

2 ______________________

Her experiment showed that, for an act of kindness to be paid forward, it must be met with **gratitude**. But what happens if the person isn't **appreciative**? Your **thoughtful gesture** might not always be accepted with a **grateful** smile. Efforts to help can be interpreted as unwanted attention. You wanted to be **helpful**, but now you just feel bad!

3 ______________________

Even if someone **appreciates** your help, how much is too much? They say kindness is its own **reward**, but research shows that a kind act will not be carried out if it is too difficult or takes too much time. There is a point at which the effort becomes greater than the reward. Paying it forward isn't as simple as it sounds.

B **Read the review again. Write the headings in the correct places.**

There are limits A chain of favors Two sides to the story

2 VOCABULARY: Describing good deeds

A 1.55 **Complete the chart with the bold words and expressions from the review. Listen and check. Which word families refer to giving help and which to receiving help?**

verb	noun	adjective	expression
help	help	______	______
	______	______	show some gratitude
	______	kind	______
think	thought	thoughtful	______
______	appreciation	______	show your appreciation
	______	rewarding	… is its own reward

B Now go to page 146. Do the vocabulary exercises for 6.2.

C GROUP WORK **Discuss the questions.**

"Kindness is its own reward." What does that mean? Do you agree? How far are you willing to go to help others? Think of something that you are willing to do and something you are not willing to do. For ideas, watch Tayra's video.

REAL STUDENT

Are your answers the same as Tayra's?

3 GRAMMAR: Passive with modals

A **Choose the correct words to complete the rules. Read the sentences in the grammar box to help you.**

1 To form the passive with a modal, use modal verb + *be* + **past / past participle**.
2 For something that is probable but not definite, use the modal ***can / might / must / will***.
3 For something that is one of many possibilities, use the modal ***can / might / must / will***.
4 For something that is definite or necessary, use the modal ***can / might / must / will***.
5 For something that is generally true in the situation, use the modal ***can / might / must / will***.

Passive with modals

An act of kindness **must be met** with gratitude.
Your gesture **might not** always **be accepted** with a smile.
Efforts to help **can be interpreted** as unwanted attention.
A kind act **will not be carried out** if it is too difficult.

B PAIR WORK **Complete the sentences with an appropriate modal verb. Sometimes more than one modal may be appropriate.**

1 If the program gets enough support, its goals ________ be achieved by the end of this year.
2 These rooms ________ be set up as a job center or a children's after-school program. We're not sure yet.
3 Unfortunately, these facilities ________ be adapted for the disabled because there is no place for an elevator.
4 Next winter, help ________ be provided to all families in need. You ________ donate used coats and blankets anytime.

C **Now go to page 135. Do the grammar exercise for 6.2.**

4 SPEAKING

A GROUP WORK **Do you agree or disagree with the statements? Why? Think of more statements to express your opinions on helping others.**

- Money should be given to charities not individuals.
- Food should be provided by local authorities for everybody who needs it.
- Our taxes should be spent on helping people in our local community.

I agree with the first statement because you never know what individuals are going to do with the money you give them.

6.3 IT'S ALL GOOD

LESSON OBJECTIVE

- offer, refuse, and accept help with something

1 FUNCTIONAL LANGUAGE

A 1.56 **Look at the picture. What is the person doing? Why is she doing it? Read and listen to the conversations. Which conversation matches the picture?**

INSIDER ENGLISH

"I insist" is a polite way to show someone that you will not change your mind.

1.56 Audio script

1 A Excuse me, **would you like to sit down?**
B Oh no, **I'm OK. Thanks anyway.**
A Please, I insist. I'm getting off at the next stop anyway.
B Well, OK. Thank you.
A No worries. Have a good day!
B You, too!

2 A You're getting really wet. **Let me share my umbrella** with you.
B Oh, **you don't have to do that.**
A I know, but it's pouring rain.
B Well, **OK then, thanks.**

3 A Well, hi there, neighbor.
B Hi, Mr. Samuels.
A **Let me give you a hand with that.**
B No, really, **I can manage.**
A Are you sure? Your hands look pretty full. Here, **let me do that.**
B Well, OK. **That's very nice of you.**
A There you go!
B **Thanks, I really appreciate it.**
A **Can I help you with** anything else?
B **Nope, it's all good.** Thanks again.

B **Complete the chart with the bold expressions from the conversations.**

Making offers	Refusing offers	Accepting offers
[1] ______ like (to sit down)?	I'm OK. Thanks [4] ______ .	OK then, thanks.
[2] ______ (share my umbrella with you).	You [5] ______ ______ to do that.	That's very [8] ______ / kind of you.
Let me give you a hand with that.	I can [6] ______ .	Thanks, I really [9] ______ it.
Can I [3] ______ you with (anything else)?	Nope, it's [7] ______ good.	

C PAIR WORK **Practice the conversations in exercise A, but change the expressions.**

Excuse me, would you like to share my umbrella?

That's very kind of you. Thank you!

2 REAL-WORLD STRATEGY

A 1.57 **Listen to the conversations. What is the situation in each? What is the difference in the outcome?**

IMPOSING ON SOMEBODY

Sometimes you have to make a request that others might not like. You can soften it by starting the request like this:

I'm sorry to have to ask, but is it OK if … ? *I don't mean to be rude, but would you mind … ?*

B 1.57 **Read the information about imposing on someone and listen again. What expressions do the people use?**

C PAIR WORK **Student A: Change one of the conversations in exercise A so that you are imposing on someone, or create a new situation of your choice. Student B: Accept or reject the request. Swap roles and have another conversation.**

I'm sorry to have to ask, but could you move over? It's difficult for me to sit in the middle with all these bags.

INSIDER ENGLISH

When someone in the back part of a line of people doesn't want to wait and moves to the front part of the line, they *cut the line* or *jump the line*.

3 PRONUNCIATION FOCUS: Saying /b/ or /v/ in the middle of a word

A 1.58 **Listen to the words. Focus on the sound of the bold letters. Practice saying them.**

/b/ um**b**rella /v/ con**v**ersation

B 1.59 **Listen. Who says the bold letter correctly? Write A or B.**

1 um**b**rella ____ 3 ha**v**e ____ 5 gi**v**e ____

2 con**v**ersation ____ 4 terri**b**le ____ 6 pro**b**lem ____

C PAIR WORK **Say the words in exercise 3B to your partner. Does your partner say the /b/ and /v/ sounds clearly?**

4 SPEAKING

A PAIR WORK **Work with a partner. Choose one of the situations and act out a conversation. Then think of a situation of your own and act out that conversation.**

1 A parent needs help going up some stairs with a stroller.

2 Somebody has dropped a lot of fruit and vegetables in the supermarket.

3 A person's car has broken down on the side of the road.

Hey, let me give you a hand with that.

Thanks! I really appreciate it.

6.4 PAINTING SAFER STREETS

LESSON OBJECTIVE

- write a report about a community project

1 LISTENING

A 1.60 LISTEN FOR GIST **Look at the picture of people painting a street. Why do you think they are doing this? Listen to the podcast to check your answers.**

Perhaps they are creating a pedestrian zone to give people a nice place to spend time.

B 1.60 LISTEN FOR DETAILS **Listen again. Answer the questions.**

1 What kind of people are involved in the intersection repair project?

2 Why do they paint the intersections in particular?

C 1.60 LISTEN FOR ATTITUDE **What is the attitude of each person who calls the show? What words do they use to describe the project? In what other ways can you detect their attitude?**

1 Eric has a positive/negative attitude about the project.
How do you know? ______

2 Isabel has a positive/negative attitude about the project.
How do you know? ______

3 Jeannette has a positive/negative attitude about the project.
How do you know? ______

D PAIR WORK THINK CRITICALLY **Discuss the questions.**

- Do you think public art is a good thing for communities and cities? Why or why not?
- Do you think there are other problems that are more important to address? What are some examples?

2 PRONUNCIATION: Listening for /j/ between words

A 1.61 **Listen to the extracts from the podcast. Listen for the /j/ sound between the underlined words.**

1 Today, we're going to Portland, Oregon, to hear about the Intersection Repair project.

2 And how was the experience?

3 Kids, the unemployed, the elderly – everyone just did whatever they could to help out.

B 1.62 **Listen. Underline the words you hear that are connected by a /j/ sound.**

1 We asked for Portlanders to call in and share their thoughts.

2 Me and my friends all worked on the project.

C **Choose the correct words to complete the statement.**

A /j/ sound is often used to connect two words when the first word *starts* / *ends* in an /i/ sound and the second word starts with a *consonant* / *vowel.*

3 WRITING

A Look at the picture of another project. What do you think the idea behind it is? Read the report to check your answer.

Vertical gardens cover the walls of art centers and apartment blocks in many cities around the world, but Mexico City is doing something more ambitious. Their "Verde Vertical" project is aimed at transforming hundreds of pillars that support overpasses into vertical gardens.

A spokesman from the company responsible for the gardens promises that pollution will be reduced and the cityscape will be improved: "We live in a very gray city, but as soon as we find a park, a green landscape, our mood changes. This is going to change people's routines."

When asked for comment, one driver said, "I drive to work every day on this road and there's a lot of traffic. It's stressful. Just seeing something green relaxes me, you know?"

However, a pedestrian disagreed: "A road is a road. They can disguise it with these plants, but it doesn't change anything."

The project aims to provide the city with an extra 40,000 meters of greenery to improve both air quality and the mood of the city's 20 million residents. The lives of those stuck in the city's traffic jams should be improved greatly – at least in theory!

GLOSSARY

overpass (*n*) a bridge that carries a road or railway over another road

B **Read the report again. What is the difference between this project and the Portland project (from exercise 1)? What do they have in common? Consider these points:**

- the people responsible for the project
- the people who benefit from the project
- the goals of the project

Which project do you prefer? Which one do you think is going to help the community more?

C WRITING SKILL **What opinions of other people are expressed in the report above? Find the phrases used to introduce these quotes and underline them.**

WRITE IT

D 1.60 **Listen again to the podcast from exercise 1. Write a short report (120–150 words) about the Portland project. Include a description of the project, how it was done, and positive and negative opinions from the callers. Be sure to introduce each quote.**

6.5 TIME TO SPEAK
Your urban art project

LESSON OBJECTIVE
- design an urban project for your community

FIND IT

A **RESEARCH** **Look at the picture and read the description. Go online to find out more if you can. Then discuss the questions.**

- What do you think is especially interesting about this art project?
- How do you think it benefits the community and its people?
- How might this project inspire others?
- Is there anything similar (in appearance or inspiration) in your area? Describe it. Find pictures online if you can.

The Morrinho Art Project is a model of a *comunidade* (neighborhood) in Rio de Janeiro. It was created by 14-year-old resident Cirlan Souza de Oliveira to show pride in his community.

B **DECIDE** **Work in small groups. Think of a space in your town or city which could benefit from urban art. Discuss these points:**

1. The place: Decide on a place in your town or city that could benefit from a project.
2. The project: What are you going to create in this space?
3. The benefits to the community: What advantages will the project bring to the community? How will that happen?

The old city walls should be restored and volunteers from each of the city's neighborhoods can create a mural that explains something about their area – a visual history of the city.

C **DISCUSS** **Work with a student from a different group. Explain your projects to each other. Suggest improvements and possible changes to the projects. Make notes to show to your group.**

D **Return to your original group and compare notes. Make any changes necessary. Identify the main points of your project, give it a name, and prepare your presentation.**

E **PRESENT** **Present your project ideas to the class. Listen to all the presentations and decide on the most effective and the most original. Be prepared to support your opinion.**

To check your progress, go to page 154.

USEFUL PHRASES

DECIDE

We're going to focus on ... (place)

We're going to create ...

The project will help the area because ...

DISCUSS

Our group decided to ...

Your project could be improved by ...

Have you thought about ... ?

PRESENT

Our project is called ...

We decided/ thought that ...

We chose to ... because ...

REVIEW 2 (UNITS 4–6)

1 VOCABULARY

A **Which word or phrase doesn't belong in each set. Circle it. Then add it to the correct set.**

Advertising: logo DJ merchandising commercial fashion statement

Jobs in the media: comedian filmmaker designer entertainer volunteer

Story types: family saga personal tragedy feel-good story slogan success story

Plans with people: get together tall tale cheer somebody up give up on somebody hang out with

Community work: donate get involved with let someone down take part in help out

B **Think of two more words or phrases that you know for each category and add them above.**

2 GRAMMAR

A **Choose the correct words to complete the paragraph.**

I love everything about France. My husband, [1]*who / that* is a doctor, is from France, and that's [2]*why / where* we spent our honeymoon. Until then, I [3]*have / had* never been abroad. Last night we [4]*supposed / were supposed* to celebrate our wedding anniversary with friends at our favorite restaurant, the *French Hall*. The restaurant [5]*is located / locates* inside the Mondrian Hotel, which [6]*is / was* founded in 1752. It [7]*must / can* be the oldest hotel in town. However, we [8]*saw / had seen* an accident on the way, and we stopped to help. When we finally [9]*arrived / had arrived* at the restaurant, all our friends [10]*were / had* already left.

B PAIR WORK **Have you ever missed a celebration? What happened?**

C PAIR WORK **Complete the sentences with the modal verbs below. Use positive or negative forms as appropriate. Compare your sentences with a partner. Do you have similar views?**

can might must should will

1 School children ______ be allowed to work.
2 If everybody helps, poverty ______ be ended in less than 20 years.
3 Elderly people ______ be sent to special homes.

3 SPEAKING

A PAIR WORK **Talk to your partner about an experience you've had this year that you had never had before. Use the questions as a guide.**

- What was the experience?
- Why did you want to do it? Why hadn't you done it before?
- What was special about it? What have you learned or gained from it?

B **What have you learned about your partner? Tell the class.**

Juan had always wanted to join a community garden, and he finally did it. He's learned to take care of plants, and he's also connected with lots of people who …

4 FUNCTIONAL LANGUAGE

A **Complete the conversations that take place at a school with the words in the box.**

can manage	don't know	find
get it	let me	must be
really think	so much	what it is

1 **A** I [1] ______________________ the new school TV commercial is fantastic.

B Yes, absolutely. And I [2] ______________________ the slogan very strong: "Unlock your door to the future."

C I [3] ______________________ . It's not [4] ______________________ that I don't like the slogan; it's just that I think it doesn't sound very modern.

2 **A** I'm sorry, but you're not in English 203. You're in English 205.

B I don't [5] ______________________ . I was supposed to be in English 203. There [6] ______________________ some kind of mistake. Can you transfer me to 203?

A I don't think that's possible. That class is full. But I can put you on a waiting list.

B Well, OK. I guess it is [7] ______________________ .

3 **A** [8] ______________________ give you a hand with those files. They look pretty heavy.

B No, really, I [9] ______________________ . But thanks anyway.

5 SPEAKING

A PAIR WORK **Choose one of the situations and act it out.**

1 A reporter has asked you and your friend about who you think the best soccer player today is. You disagree with each other.

A As I see it, (name of player) is the best soccer player this year.

B Sorry, I really don't agree …

2 You made a hotel reservation, but the receptionist can't find it. React and ask for a solution.

A I'm sorry, but we don't have a reservation in that name …

B There must be some kind of mistake …

3 You see an elderly person who is having problems putting something in their car. Offer to help.

A Can I help you with that?

B No, really, I can manage.

B **Change roles and repeat the role play.**

1.1 TENSE REVIEW (SIMPLE AND CONTINUOUS) (PAGE 3)

SIMPLE TENSES			
Simple present			
I get up at 8. He gets up at 8.	I don't get up at 8. He doesn't get up at 8	Do you get up at 8? Does he get up at 8?	Yes, I do. / No, I don't Yes, he does. / No, he doesn't.
Simple past			
I went to work 8.	I didn't go to work.	Did you go to work?	Yes, I did. / No, I didn't.
Present perfect			
I've done this before. He's done this before.	I haven't done this before. He hasn't done this before.	Have you ever done this before? Has he ever done this before?	Yes, I have. / No, I haven't. Yes, he has. / No, he hasn't.

CONTINUOUS TENSES			
Present continuous			
I'm reading. You're reading She's reading.	I'm not reading. You aren't reading. She isn't reading.	Are you reading? Is she reading?	Yes, I am. / No, I'm not. Yes, she is. / No, she isn't.
Past continuous			
I was eating. You were eating. It was eating.	I wasn't eating. You weren't eating. It wasn't eating.	Were you eating? Was it eating?	Yes, I was. / No, I wasn't. Yes, it was. / No, it wasn't.
Present perfect continuous			
I've been waiting. He's been waiting.	I haven't been waiting. He hasn't been waiting.	Have you been waiting? Has he been waiting?	Yes, I have. / No, I haven't. Yes, he has. / No, he hasn't.

A **Choose the correct form of the verb.**

1 Every day *I'm getting up / I get up* at 7 a.m.
2 Yesterday I *wasn't going / didn't go* to work.
3 *I'm painting / I paint* my bedroom at the moment.
4 *I've been standing / I've stood* here for half an hour waiting for the bus!
5 I was just sitting down to eat dinner when the phone *was ringing / rang*.
6 Have you *ever visited / been visiting* New York in the winter?

1.2 DYNAMIC AND STATIVE VERBS (PAGE 5)

Stative and dynamic verbs

Dynamic verbs describe actions (*go, sleep, talk*). They can be used in the continuous form to describe:

- an action in progress: I**'m working** on a community art project.
- a plan: I**'m interviewing** three candidates tomorrow.

Stative verbs are generally not used with continuous forms. They describe:

- personal qualities (*be*): They**'re** responsible. She**'s** polite.
- preferences (*like, love, hate, want, need*): We **need** someone who's polite. She **wants** to be successful.
- opinions (*believe, think*): I **think** we have the right person.

Most verbs can be dynamic or stative, depending on the context.

Dynamic	Stative
She**'s being** very careful.	She**'s** very responsible.
I**'m thinking** of looking for a new job.	I **think** curiosity is a good quality.
I**'m having** lunch with her tomorrow.	I **have** too much to do.

Stative verbs that describe mental activity *(know, understand, want, need)* are always stative.

A **Check (✓) the sentences that use dynamic and stative verbs correctly. Correct the incorrect ones. Why are they incorrect?**

- ☐ **1** I'm being very scared of snakes.
- ☐ **2** He's being very responsible about his studies.
- ☐ **3** I'm not really seeing what you mean.
- ☐ **4** I'm seeing Jon on Saturday.
- ☐ **5** I'm loving every minute of this holiday.
- ☐ **6** I'm liking to take it easy on the weekend.

2.1 REAL CONDITIONALS (PAGE 13)

Real conditional sentences

Conditional sentences are made up of two parts: the condition (*if* clause) and the result. The clauses can go in either order. When the condition comes first, use a comma to separate it from the result.

If + present, present

Use *if* + present, present to talk about a possible situation and to describe general truths, facts, and habits.

Condition	Result
Even **if** a vegetable **doesn't look** good,	Chef Barber **makes** it taste great.

If + present, imperative

Use *if* + present, imperative to tell someone what to do.

Condition	Result
If it **tastes** good,	**eat** it!

If + present, *will / be going to / might*

Use *if* + present, *will / be going to / might* to talk about possible future results.

Condition	Result
If you **prefer** flavor to good looks,	you**'ll** love his food.
If you **like** good food,	you**'re going to** love Chef Barber's restaurant.
If Chef Barber **serves** it,	I **might** try it.

A Check (✓) the sentences that are correct. Correct the ones with errors.

- [ ] 1 If you like trendy restaurants, you go to Maxine's Bistro.
- [ ] 2 If enough people start eating quinoa, it is going to be the next big thing.
- [ ] 3 If a restaurant is "zero waste," doesn't throw away food.
- [ ] 4 If more people will eat at zero waste restaurants, it will help solve world hunger.
- [ ] 5 People lose interest if a restaurant will not try something new.
- [ ] 6 If something is all the rage, it is fashionable.

2.2 CLAUSES WITH *AFTER*, *UNTIL*, *WHEN* (PAGE 15)

A **Correct the mistakes in the bold verbs.**

1 Of course, before you**'ll make** the recipe you'll need to go shopping.

2 When the guests **will arrive** at 8, we'll need to have everything ready, so get organized now.

3 The flight takes about three hours, so when we land, it **is** 6:30.

4 When the fog **will clear,** we'll be able to leave.

5 Once you**'ll get** used to the job, it'll be a lot easier.

6 Until you**'re going to have** all the papers, you won't be allowed to apply for the position.

3.1 *TOO* AND *ENOUGH* (PAGE 23)

too* and *enough

	too	***enough***
with nouns	My commute took **too much time.**	We don't have **enough time.**
with adjectives	I was **too busy.**	The suburban lifestyle wasn't **exciting enough.**
with adverbs	I have to work **too hard.**	He doesn't work **hard enough.**
with verbs	My apartment **costs too much.**	I don't **earn enough.**

A **Add *too* or *enough* to the sentences below.**

1 I'm sorry, I can't go out tonight. I have ^too much work to do.

2 Oh no, I don't have money! Can you buy the ticket for me?

3 I'm sorry, we can't serve you. It's late. The kitchen is already closed.

4 Is he old to drive? He looks very young.

5 You work hard! You need to take a break.

6 There aren't hours in the day to do everything!

7 There are many people waiting in line. I'm going to come back later.

8 Is that hot for you or would you like me to heat it up in the microwave?

3.2 MODIFYING COMPARISONS (PAGE 25)

Modifying comparative adjectives.		
It's	a whole lot way a bit a little	easier (than something else).
Modifying comparative structures		
It's	just nearly almost nowhere near	as expensive as (the other one).
Modifying superlative adjectives.		
It's	**by far**	the (best coffee).

A **Add one word to modify the comparisons in the sentences. Sometimes more than one answer is possible.**

1 Ian is ______________ as tall as his older brother James!

2 That was by ______________ the hardest test I've ever taken!

3 It's really difficult to choose between them. I guess this one is a ______________ cheaper.

4 I'm sorry, but this movie is nowhere ______________ as good as the last one she made.

5 I prefer this one. I think it's a ______________ nicer.

4.1 MODALS OF SPECULATION (PAGE 35)

Modals expressing certainty	
This **must** be an authentic jersey.	This **must not** be an authentic jersey. This **can't** be an authentic jersey.
Modal expressing uncertainty	
This **may** be an authentic jersey. This **might** be an authentic jersey. This **could** be an authentic jersey.	This **may not** be an authentic jersey. This **might not** be an authentic jersey.

A **Rewrite the sentences with modal verbs so that they have the same meaning.**

1 It's easy to imagine that American football becomes more popular in Europe.

American football could easily become more popular in Europe.

2 I'm sure that Chelsea won't win the league this year.

____

3 It's possible that more NBA teams will put sponsors on their shirts.

____

4 I'm sure that Real Madrid has the most fans of any team in Spain.

____

5 I'm sure that soccer is the world's most popular sport.

____

6 I'm sure that tennis is not as popular as soccer.

____

4.2 SUBJECT AND OBJECT RELATIVE CLAUSES (PAGE 37)

Subject relative clauses

In subject relative clauses, the *relative pronoun* is the subject of the relative clause and is always followed by a verb.

Small stories ***that / which*** **grow into something bigger** are found all over the internet.

The young boy ***who / that*** **made his own Messi jersey** captured the world's attention.

Object relative clauses

In object relative clauses, the *relative pronoun* is the object of the relative clause and is always followed by a noun or pronoun.

He met the man **(*who / that*) he admired more than anyone else**.

Viral stories can be big stories **(*that / which*) we share with the world**.

He got to travel to Qatar ***where*** **his dreams came true.**

In object relative clauses the relative pronouns *that*, *which*, and *who* can be omitted.

A **Read the sentences and circle the relative pronouns. Cross them out where they can be omitted.**

1 She's a filmmaker who I really like. She made a film about robots who control our lives.
2 That's the guitar that I bought in Spain. The little music shop where I bought it was so cool!
3 I have a friend who designs amazing clothes. She's someone that I met in college.
4 LeBron James is an example of an athlete who has become an icon.
5 Comedians are the celebrities that I find most interesting.

5.1 PAST PERFECT (PAGE 45)

Past perfect

To form the past perfect use *had* and a past participle.

She **hadn't shown** her stories to anybody.

Use the past perfect to talk about things that happened before another event in the past.

The previous owners **had died** mysteriously before we moved in.

(The first owners died, then we moved in sometime later.)

When there are two completed events in the past, use the simple past for the more recent event.

I'd never written a novel. I had no idea where to start.

Questions and short answers

Had he ever **written** a novel? Yes, he **had**. / No, he **hadn't**.

A **Complete the conversations with the verbs in parentheses ( ) in the past perfect or the simple past.**

1 A How [1] was (be) your vacation?
B Great! We went skiing. I [2] ______ (never ski) before!
A [3] ______ (you/ever visit) that area before?
B No, it [4] ______ (be) my first time.

2 A [5] ______ (you/ have) a good meeting?
B Not really. When I [6] ______ (arrive) at the office, the meeting [7] ______ (already begin).
A Was the boss there?
B Yes. He [8] ______ (arrive) long before anyone else.

5.2 *WAS/WERE GOING TO; WAS/WERE SUPPOSED TO* (PAGE 47)

was/were going to; was/were supposed to

These forms describe an action that was planned in the past. They are often used to say that a plan didn't happen.

We **were going to** get together, but she texted to say she couldn't come.

We **were supposed to** get together, but she texted to say that she couldn't come.

They are often followed by *but* + an explanation of why the plan didn't happen.

Affirmative	Negative	Question
We **were going to** see a movie (but we didn't).	We **weren't going to** see a movie (but we did).	**Were** you **going to** see a movie?
I **was supposed to** work last weekend (but I didn't).	You **weren't supposed to** work last weekend (but you did).	**Was** he **supposed to** work last weekend?

A **Complete the sentences with the words in parentheses ( ).**

1 My parents ________________ (supposed/move) into their new house last week. They ________________ (going/leave) their old place on Friday, but there was a problem.

2 Some friends and I ________________ (going/visit) some other friends in Florida. We ________________ (suppose/drive) down on Sunday night, but there was a terrible storm and we couldn't leave until Tuesday morning.

3 I ________________ (not supposed/work) this weekend. I ________________ (going/stay) home and relax, but there was an emergency at the hospital, so I had to go in.

4 **A** ________________ (you/supposed/have) a big test this week?

B Yes, we ________________ (going/take) it tomorrow, but they canceled it.

6.1 PRESENT AND PAST PASSIVE (PAGE 55)

Present and past passive

Use passive verb forms to focus on an action, rather than on who or what performs the action.

We use *by* to say who or what does the action in a passive sentence.

The cafés are used by lots of people in the community.

Sometimes we use the passive if the person who does the action is not known or is not important.

These dogs and cats were abandoned in our neighborhood.

The object of the active sentence is the subject of the passive sentence.

Lots of people use these **cafés.** ➔ These **cafés** are used by lots of people.

A **Change the sentences from active to passive.**

1 People usually donate a lot of money to charities that help animals.

____

2 They founded the organization in 1976.

____

3 Licensed professionals train volunteers to help elderly people in the community.

____

4 At first, the charity devoted most of its funds to conserving wildlife.

____

6.2 PASSIVES WITH MODALS (PAGE 57)

A **Change the sentences to passive. Use an appropriate modal.**

1 It's possible that soon the government will introduce new laws about climate change.

____

2 Climate change will alter our behavior.

____

3 It's possible to make positive changes if we all work together.

____

4 They are going to give him an award for all his charity work, it's certain.

____

5 It's probable that people will view this decision in a negative way.

____

This page is intentionally left blank

VOCABULARY PRACTICE

1.1 DESCRIBING ACCOMPLISHMENTS (PAGE 2)

A **Match the stories to phrases from the box. Some may have more than one correct answer.**

break a record	face your fear	~~get a lot of likes~~
have a sense of humor	run a business	set a goal for yourself
take pride in something	tell a joke	win a medal

1 I posted a funny picture of myself on Instagram and all my friends liked it.
get a lot of likes, ____________________

2 I hate speaking in front of people. It really scares me. But last week I gave a short presentation to a room of 70 people, and it went well.
____

3 I'm going to learn to speak German by the end of this year.
____

4 He ran the race in the fastest time ever.
____

5 Matt's new girlfriend is so much fun. She makes me laugh all the time!
____

6 My brother has a small art supplies store in town. He's so proud of it!
____

B **Complete the sentences with the phrases in the box. Change them as needed to fit the sentence.**

~~rise to a challenge~~	run a marathon	run a business
set a goal for yourself	win a medal	work with your hands

1 Your new job sounds difficult, but I'm sure you will *rise to the challenge* .
2 My sister is an artist. She makes sculptures. She really likes to ____________________ .
3 My brother loves running. Last year, he ____________________ for charity.
4 My grandfather was an Olympic athlete. He once ____________________ for swimming.
5 I have always wanted to ____________________ . It must be great to be your own boss!
6 I have ____________________ of learning a new language. I think I'll try Japanese!

1.2 DESCRIBING KEY QUALITIES (PAGE 4)

A **Choose the correct word.**

1 Tom is so *curious / curiosity* about everything. He never stops asking questions!
2 Her uncle is a very *successful / success* lawyer. He has worked on some very important cases.
3 He isn't very *ambition / ambitious*. I mean, he doesn't want a promotion or a better job or anything.
4 She's an *experienced / experience* actor. She's been working in theater for more than 30 years.
5 I think *truthful / truthfulness* is such an important quality in a person. I hate it when people lie!
6 They're always so positive about everything. I love their *enthusiastic / enthusiasm*.

B **Complete the sentences with the correct form of the words in the box.**

confident	creativity	independence	polite	qualified	responsible

1 Dog owners must be ready to take ______ for their pets and always clean up after them.

2 I think it's so important to teach children the basic rules of ______ , like saying "please" and "thank you."

3 I was really ______ as a child. I always wanted to do everything for myself.

4 It takes a lot of ______ to start your own business. You really have to believe in yourself.

5 She came up with a really ______ solution to the problem. It was so original – and it worked!

6 For this job, we need someone with a college degree, a special certificate, and experience! How will we ever find someone with all the right ______ ?

2.1 DESCRIBING TRENDS (PAGE 12)

A **Complete the sentences with the correct expression. The first word is given to help you. Which sentences do you disagree with? Change them to make them true for you.**

1 The raw diet, where you only eat raw foods, seems to be *on* ______ , but maybe it will *come* ______ in a few years.

2 Food trucks are really *gaining* ______ . They might *be* ______ !

3 Nearly everyone loves pizza. It will never *go* ______ .

4 Have you been to Chef Cesar's new restaurant? It's *all* ______ .

5 Many diets are just *a* ______ . They are popular for a while, but then people *lose* ______ .

B **Choose the correct words to complete the paragraph.**

What is healthy anymore?

Japanese food is suddenly [1]*all the rage / going out of style*. It seems that every restaurant in my town offers a sushi or sashimi now. It's [2]*gaining / losing* popularity because a lot of its ingredients are raw, and they say uncooked food is good for you. Meanwhile, people are [3]*gaining / losing* interest in Argentinian restaurants because cooked meat is supposed to be bad for your heart. But what is healthy anymore? The experts change their minds all the time. You never know what the [4]*old-fashioned / next big* thing will be.

2.2 PREPARING FOOD (PAGE 14)

A **Choose the correct word to complete the sentences.**

1 *Garlic / Mint* has a strong taste – don't kiss anyone after eating it.

2 *Pineapple / Eggplant* makes a really nice dessert.

3 You can add *mint / shrimp* to tea for a refreshing drink.

4 Before you eat any vegetables you should really *stir / rinse* them.

5 It's not a good idea to *fry / boil* all your food, it's very fatty.

6 You can *barbecue / chop* meat or seafood outside on the grill – it's delicious.

B **Complete the paragraph with words from the box. More than one option is sometimes possible. There are two extra words.**

boil	chop	eggplant	fry	garlic
ginger	shrimp	stir	zucchini	

Not sure what to make for dinner tonight? Curry might just be the answer. This Indian dish is both delicious and easy to make. All you need are a few vegetables, a few spices, and maybe meat, fish, or beans for protein. My favorite curries are very spicy and use a lot of [1] ____________. For vegetables, I usually use potatoes and carrots. But you can use [2] ____________ or [3] ____________ – just be sure to [4] ____________ your vegetables in cold water before you [5] ____________ them. Most of my curries are vegetarian, but I'll occasionally add some seafood – usually [6] ____________. The actual cooking part is easy – just add everything to a hot pan and [7] ____________ it all together!

3.1 TALKING ABOUT TIME AND MONEY (PAGE 22)

A **Complete the paragraph with the words in the box.**

balance	cost of living	lifestyle	salary cut	trade	value	worth

The [1] ____________ is generally much lower in smaller towns – big cities are much more expensive! It's also much easier to find a healthy work/life [2] ____________, although you will probably have to take a [3] ____________ if you decide to move out of the city. You will also need to [4] ____________ the fast-paced city [5] ____________ for a quieter life. If you [6] ____________ peace and quiet, clean air, and living closer to nature, you'll probably find that it's [7] ____________ it.

B **Do you agree with the ideas in the paragraph in exercise A? Complete these sentences about your hometown. Give examples.**

1 The cost of living is generally …
2 The standard of living is generally …
3 It's easy/difficult to find a good work/life balance because …
4 It's easy/difficult to boost your career chances because …
5 I really value the … in my town.
6 I can/can't afford to … because …

3.2 TALKING ABOUT PRICES AND VALUE (PAGE 24)

A **Choose the correct verb.**

1 I know I can *take advantage of / rely on* them to give me great service.
2 I've just *come up with / made the most of* a great idea for a new business!
3 I'm going to *invest in / treat myself to* a trip to a spa next weekend.
4 How much do they usually *charge for / pay a fair price for* a meal for two?
5 I might go with you. It *depends on / has an effect on* how money I can save by then.

B **Complete each question with the correct preposition. Then write answers to the questions.**

1 What has the biggest effect ____________ your quality of life, your job or your social life?
2 Do you think it's better to invest ____________ property or education?
3 Do you think your quality of life depends more ____________ time or money?
4 Do you make the most ____________ your free time, or do you waste it?
5 Do you ever treat yourself ____________ an expensive meal?

4.1 TALKING ABOUT ADVERTISING (PAGE 35)

A Choose the best option to complete the sentences.

1 The Apple *sponsor / logo* is one of the most recognizable in the world.
2 "Finger lickin' good" is the *product / slogan* of a famous fast food chain.
3 Many smaller companies can't afford to *advertise / sponsor* their products on TV.
4 I only buy one *product / brand* of jeans. They're my absolute favorite.
5 Mike wears the most usual outfits. He says he wants to make a *fashion statement / commercial.*

B Complete the quotes with the words in the box.

advertisement	brand	fashion statement	logo
merchandise	products	slogan	

Nike is my favorite [1] ______________ of shoe. I like their swoosh [2] ______________ and their [3] ______________, "Just do it!" I love wearing their [4] ______________. I think it makes a real [5] ______________.

Really? Personally, I don't like to wear [6] ______________ with the company's logo on it. It's like being a walking [7] ______________ for the company.

4.2 TALKING ABOUT PEOPLE IN THE MEDIA (PAGE 37)

A Complete the sentences with words from the box. Some sentences may have more than one correct answer.

audience	celebrity	comedian	designer	DJ	entertainer
filmmaker	hero	icon	model	performer	producer

1 I would never want to be a ______________. There's too much attention from the media.
2 Guillermo del Toro is probably my favorite ______________. He was the director and the ______________ of *The Shape of Water.*
3 We didn't have a band for our wedding. We just hired a ______________.
4 Being a professional ______________, like a musician, would be hard because they have to travel so much.
5 One of my favorite events in New York is Fashion Week. I love to see all the ______________ wearing the latest designs.
6 Ralph Lauren is a famous ______________. He founded the clothing brand Polo.
7 My sister really likes that ______________ but I don't. His jokes can be a little mean.
8 Steph Curry is more than just an athlete. He's an ______________.
9 In most of his films, he plays a ______________. But in my favorite film, he's the bad guy.
10 I'd never want to be a ______________ on stage. What if the ______________ didn't like my act?

5.1 DESCRIBING STORIES (PAGE 44)

A Read the news headlines and decide which story types they probably are. More than one type is possible.

coming-of-age story	family saga	feel-good story	hard-luck story
horror story	human interest story	love story	mystery
personal tragedy	success story	tall tale	tearjerker

1 Teenager discovers possible cure for cancer ______
2 New York couple celebrates 86 years of marriage ______
3 Dog finds family after 3-day adventure ______
4 Family loses home in forest fire ______
5 Panda gives birth to twins in Toronto zoo ______

B Read the sentences from different stories. What kinds of stories do you think they are?

1 He became the first man to climb to the top of Mt. Everest solo! ______
2 One wrong decision and he had lost everything. ______
3 As she walked forward to receive her diploma, she looked out at the three generations that had carried her to this moment. ______
4 Then, out of nowhere, an enormous bird flew down and grabbed the fish right out of my hands! So I can't show you, but it was the biggest fish anyone ever caught in that lake! Really! ______

5.2 MAKING AND BREAKING PLANS (PAGE 46)

A Choose the correct verb to complete the sentences.

1 His parents had *gone ahead / cheered up / split up* the year before, so he lived with his grandmother for a while.
2 It had been a long, hard week, and I was *ending up / looking forward to / making up* the weekend.
3 We were *held up / let down / messed up* in traffic, and we didn't get there in time.
4 He made a terrible mistake, but I wasn't ready to *give up on / look forward to / hang out with* him yet. I'd give him one more chance.

B Choose the best phrasal verb for each situation. More than one option may be correct. Write a sentence based on the situation and use at least one of the phrasal verbs you chose.

be held up	cheer up	end up
get together	give up on	go ahead
hang out with	let someone down	look forward to
make up	mess up	split up

1 He called me and said he couldn't play tennis with me this weekend. I was very disappointed.
2 She told me she had an exam next week, but I knew it wasn't true.
3 The lead singer left, and the band stopped playing together.
4 I am so mad at him! He said he wasn't feeling well, but I know he just wanted the day off.
5 I was in a hurry, but as I was leaving the office, the phone rang and I had to decide to answer it or not.
6 My friends and I try to see each other at least once a month if we can.

6.1 DISCUSSING GOOD WORKS (PAGE 54)

A Complete the sentences with the verbs and verb phrases in the box.

bring together	connect with	donate	get involved with
help out	join	take part in	volunteer

1 Every year, I ______________ some money to a particular charity.
2 It's good to ______________ a club because it gets you out of the house.
3 I don't like belonging to clubs because I don't easily ______________ other people.
4 I like to ______________ in many different activities.
5 I don't belong to the organization, but I ______________ when I have time.
6 I'd like to ______________ for things more often, but I don't have time.
7 The best way to ______________ groups is through the Internet.
8 This English class ______________ lots of different people with a common goal.

B Choose the correct words to complete the text about community action.

In Whitman County, we estimate that there are 14,000 people living in poverty. There are many ways you can help [1]*take care of / take part in* these people. First, with the food banks, you can [2]*connect / volunteer* either to pick up food donations or make deliveries. Then there's emergency housing. In this case, it's important to [3]*bring together / get to know* the needs of local people to identify and design an action plan. After some time, you can [4]*pass on / get involved in* your knowledge to new volunteers. If you're not able to give your time, you can [5]*donate / join* blankets, clothing, and appliances. Whatever you do, you are [6]*passing on / getting to know* the people in your community and making a difference.

6.2 DESCRIBING GOOD DEEDS (PAGE 56)

A Choose the best adjective to complete the sentences.

1 Helping people in need can be a very *grateful / rewarding* experience.
2 Most people are very *appreciative / thoughtful* when you do a good deed for them.
3 It's easy to lend someone a *kind / helping* hand.
4 If you don't want to seem *ungrateful / appreciative*, thank a person for what they have done for you.
5 Going to visit someone in the hospital is a very *helping / kind* thing to do.
6 Sending flowers when someone dies is a very *rewarding / thoughtful* gesture.

B Use words and phrases from the box to complete the conversations. One will not be used.

appreciate	help	helpful	thoughtful
lend a helping hand		show some gratitude	

1 **A** If you need some ______________ don't hesitate to call me!"
B Ok, I will! Thanks a lot!
2 **A** Mike never said "Thank you" after you helped him?
B No! I mean he could at least ______________ .
3 **A** It's just a small present, nothing big.
B Still, it's very ______________ . Thank you.
4 **A** This map is in French!
B Well, that's not very ______________ . We'd better ask someone for directions.
5 **A** I just wanted to tell you how much I ______________ all your help this week.
B Hey, what are friends for, right?

PROGRESS CHECK

Can you do these things? Check (✓) what you can do. Then write your answers in your notebook.

UNIT 1

Now I can ...	Prove it
☐ use expressions to talk about personal achievements.	Write five verb + noun combinations to describe someone's achievements.
☐ use a variety of simple and continuous verb forms.	Write five sentences about yourself using five different verb forms.
☐ use nouns and adjectives to talk about key qualities employers look for.	Write three pairs of words to describe yourself in ways that would appeal to a possible employer.
☐ use dynamic and stative verbs to talk about actions, habits, and states.	Complete the sentences: *I love* ________. *I'm loving* ________.
☐ make and respond to introductions.	Respond to the introduction in three different ways: *Hey, have you met Simone?*
☐ write a comment in response to an article.	Look at your comment from lesson 1.4. Can you make it better? Find three ways.

UNIT 2

Now I can ...	Prove it
☐ use expressions to describe trends.	Write four different ways to refer to something that is currently popular and four more for something unpopular.
☐ use real conditionals.	Write four sentences using *if* clauses: two to refer to a fact that is generally true and two for a future possibility.
☐ use the correct words to describe food preparation.	Describe a dish you can make in six simple steps.
☐ refer to the future with time clauses using *after, until,* and *when.*	Complete the sentences so that they are true for you: *When I finish class today,* ________. *I won't get home until* ________. *I'm going to* ________ *after I leave class today.*
☐ make, accept, and refuse offers in social situations.	Make an offer of food and/or drink, and practice different way of accepting and refusing it.
☐ write the results of a survey that you conducted.	Look at your survey results summary from lesson 2.4. Can you make it better? Find three ways.

UNIT 3

Now I can ...	Prove it
☐ use expressions to talk about time and money.	Write five phrases about time and money.
☐ use (*not*) *too* and (*not*) *enough* to talk about quantity.	Write five sentences about yourself using different structures with *too* and *enough*.
☐ use verb phrases to talk about prices and value.	Write three verb phrases, with the correct prepositions, about prices and value.
☐ use modifiers in comparisons.	Make these comparisons stronger: *It's the best movie I've ever seen. Theirs is bigger than ours.*
☐ apologize for damaging or losing someone's property and respond to an apology.	Apologize for losing something that you borrowed. Respond to the apology.
☐ write a product review.	Look at your product review from lesson 3.4. Can you make it better? Find three ways.

PROGRESS CHECK

Can you do these things? Check (✓) what you can do. Then write your answers in your notebook.

UNIT 4

Now I can …	Prove it
☐ use specific words to talk about ads and advertising.	Choose a product and discuss its brand and the different ways it is advertised.
☐ make different types of speculations using modals.	Write five sentences about something uncertain using different modal verbs for degrees of possibility.
☐ talk about different people in the media.	Talk about some recent viral news or a celebrity of current interest.
☐ use pronouns in subject and object relative clauses.	Talk about a few celebrities and describe who they are and what they do using relative clauses.
☐ exchange and discuss opinions.	Give your opinion about a current movie and then emphatically disagree with it.
☐ write a response to a post about businesses in your community.	Look at your response from lesson 4.4. Can you make it better? Find three ways.

UNIT 5

Now I can …	Prove it
☐ use specific terms to describe different types of stories.	Name five movies or books and explain what story type(s) each of them is.
☐ order events in the past using past perfect tense.	Write six things that happened yesterday. Connect events using the past perfect tense.
☐ use expressions to talk about making and breaking plans.	Write four excuses for canceling plans at the last minute.
☐ use *was/were going to* and *was/were supposed to* for canceled plans.	Complete the sentence: *I* ______________ *make dinner for us, but the electricity is out in my building!*
☐ react appropriately to problems and disappointing news.	Present a situation that involves a problem and react to it. Then resolve it or accept the situation politely.
☐ write a formal apology from a company.	Look at your apology from lesson 5.4. Can you make it better? Find three ways.

UNIT 6

Now I can …	Prove it
☐ use verbs and verb phrases to describe good works.	Describe one type of volunteer work using different verbs and verb phrases.
☐ use the passive voice in the simple present and simple past.	Write as least five sentences in passive voice to describe a charity or community group.
☐ use expressions and different forms of words to talk about good deeds.	Write six sentences about the value of doing good deeds: three about giving help and three about receiving help.
☐ use the passive voice with the modals *can, might, must,* and *will.*	Complete the instruction: *Requests for shift changes* ______________ ______________ (approve) *by the manager.*
☐ offer, refuse, and accept help.	Ask for help with something. Respond to the help that is or is not given.
☐ write a report about a community project.	Look at your report from lesson 6.4. Can you make it better? Find three ways.

PAIR WORK PRACTICE (STUDENT A)

2.5 EXERCISE A (PAGE 20) STUDENT A

Chow Mein Tacos

A small, family-run restaurant specializing in tacos. The idea is a fusion of Chinese and Mexican food, but it is not one thing or another. They don't have the right Mexican sauces or ingredients, and guests don't think the combination works. The decoration and music is also a mixture, so people don't really know what to expect of the food. They find that the tastes interfere with each other: guacamole doesn't go with sweet and sour chicken, for example. The seating area is cramped and hot in summer and the acoustics are not good. However, there is outdoor space that could be used.

GLOSSARY

cramped (*adj*) without enough space

acoustics (*n*) the qualities of a room that make it easy or difficult for people to hear

5.5 EXERCISE B (PAGE 52) STUDENT A

1 **Look at the pictures to learn about his story. Answer the questions.**

1 What plans did the man have?
2 What happened to his friend?
3 What happened while the man was waiting?

2 **Prepare to tell your story to someone from Group B.**

PAIR WORK PRACTICE

6.1 EXERCISE 4A (PAGE 55) STUDENT A

The World Wide Fund for Nature was founded in 1961. It's an international organization whose mission is to help finance other wildlife protection programs. The WWF headquarters is located based in Switzerland, but it has operations worldwide. It receives funding from a variety of sources: governments, corporate sponsors, and private donations.

5.5 EXERCISE D (PAGE 52) ALL STUDENTS

She called her own phone. He heard it ring and picked it up. Half an hour later, they met and he gave back her phone. That was the beginning of a beautiful relationship. A year later, to the day, they got married!

PAIR WORK PRACTICE (STUDENT B)

2.5 EXERCISE A (PAGE 20) STUDENT B

Veggie Heaven

A vegetarian restaurant downtown which is both take out and eat in. It's very busy at lunchtime, but people complain about the slow service, the food quality, and the prices. Foods are too heavy, there too many lentil and rice dishes. Many sandwiches and salads are pre-packaged and lose their freshness quickly. There is confusion between vegetarian and vegan dishes, with some take-out meals having the wrong labels. They have great juices, but they take a long time to make and are expensive.

GLOSSARY

heavy *(adj)* large in amount or solid and not enjoyable

5.5 EXERCISE B (PAGE 52) STUDENT B

1 **Look at the pictures to learn about her story. Answer the questions.**

1 Where was the woman at 3:00 p.m.?

2 What happened when she got home?

3 What idea did she have at 4:00 p.m.?

2 **Prepare to tell your story to someone from Group B.**

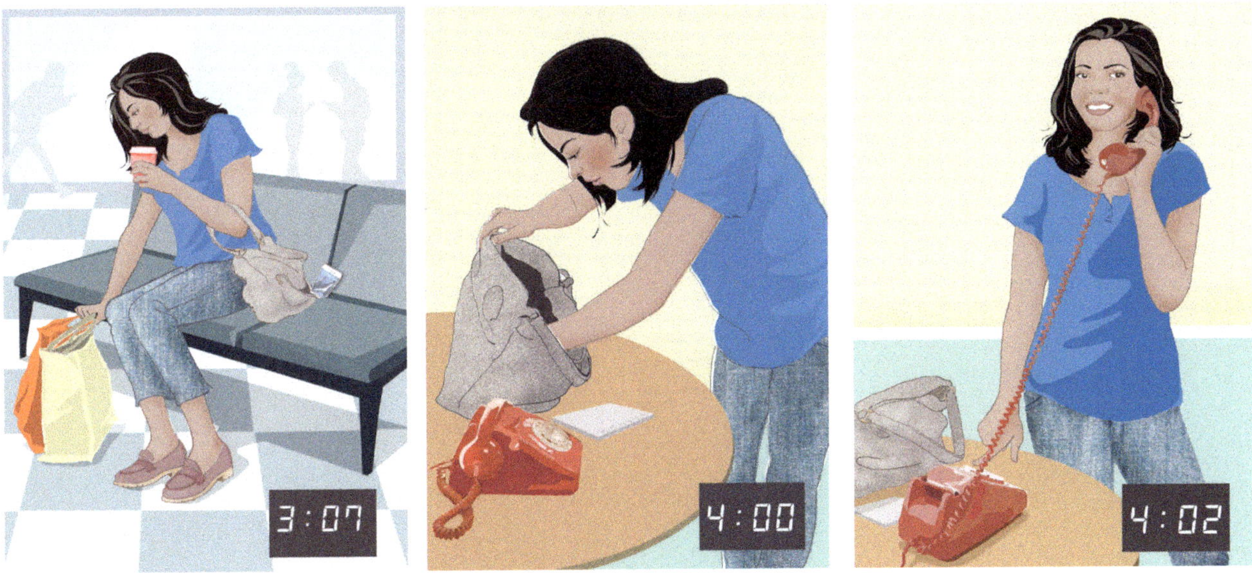

6.1 EXERCISE 4A (PAGE 55) STUDENT B

Médecins Sans Frontières, known as "Doctors Without Borders" in English, is devoted to providing medical care in war zones and in developing countries. The program first began in 1971 and now operates in over 70 nations. Although it does not have a headquarters, the program's international council meets in Geneva, Switzerland. Doctors Without Borders in almost entirely funded by private donations.

This page is intentionally left blank

This page is intentionally left blank

This page is intentionally left blank

This page is intentionally left blank

This page is intentionally left blank

This page is intentionally left blank

This page is intentionally left blank